To

Father Talbot,

who, from the start, so
graciously befriended
the "Apostles" and me

with gratitude and all
best wishes, from

Helen Walker Homan

BY POST TO THE
A P O S T L E S

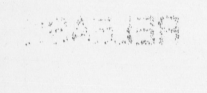

HELEN WALKER HOMAN

BY POST TO THE

APOSTLES

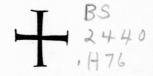

MINTON, BALCH & COMPANY

NEW YORK

To my Father,

JAMES BLAINE WALKER

MANUFACTURED IN THE UNITED STATES OF AMERICA
AT THE VAN REES PRESS

FOREWORD

Dear Reader:

Perhaps I assume too much in addressing you. Perhaps (though Heaven forbid!) you do not even exist. Yet for your sake, to say nothing of mine, I sincerely hope you do. And also, since I write you this letter, that you will not object. I hasten to tell you that I have already written letters to the Apostles and Evangelists, and they have not objected—that is, to date. But then again, they may—as alas, also may you. So I'd like to hurry on, before any of you have time to think it over.

Hastily then, dear Reader, I wish you would ask me just how I came to write these letters—for frankly, I am consumed with eagerness to tell you. And if you should first murmur that any attempt at correspondence with great Saints flavors of disrespect, I shall retort that it is certainly more respectful to write to august personages than to force an audience and speak to them. And since the sons and daughters of all Christian centuries have been guilty of the latter every time they've said their prayers, I don't see why the more formal method of addressing such personages by letter should be regarded with a lifted eye-

v

brow. Indeed, I should be grateful if you would lower yours at once, dear Reader.... That's better. Now you really look very charming again.

For that matter, why shouldn't you? Have you never realized that you actually share a great deal in common with those utterly charming persons, the Apostles? For I take it (until proved to the contrary) that you are human; and certainly, they were gloriously human ... which, whether you like the paradox or not, was what made them so gloriously holy. But has it never seemed to you, as it has to me, that the world is prone to forget their humanness in their holiness? Yet only if we recognize the former can we truly appreciate the latter in all its grandeur.

Unworthy I wanted very much to appreciate it . . . and so, myself led by their leader, Saint Peter (whose humanness even the blindest reader of the New Testament must recognize) to the suspicion that his colleagues must also have been human, I began to pry shamelessly into their private lives. It has been the most wonderful adventure of my own inconsequential existence.

If you are still listening, I should like to relate how it took me first into a new and somehow different reading of the Gospels. Read always before for their holiness, they revealed when read for their humanness a magnificent new proportion—a proportion that somehow enlarged and completed that one-

dimensional vision I had glimpsed for so many years. I cannot tell you with what anticipations of pleasure, to be fulfilled a hundredfold, I went on, in the same manner, to the Acts of the Apostles; to the Epistles of Saint Paul and Saint Peter, Saint John, Saint James, and Saint Jude; to the Apocalypse of Saint John; to the early Church Fathers—and finally, to the Apocrypha themselves, to fact and to fable—to the religious lore of ancient East and modern West. Among books of the latter, I am particularly indebted to that delightful volume, "The Glorious Company," by Tracy D. Mygatt and Frances Witherspoon. As I searched for, and found in all these, the human characteristics of that humble handful of men who, on that long-ago time, threw in their lot with Christ and, unarmed and poor, conquered the world, I came (no doubt presumptuously) to regard them as my dearest friends. Friends not dead an æon ago, but living as they had never, at least for me, lived before—as eager today as they were in the first century to spread His Divine Message over the world.

Have you ever had that particular adventure, at once so thrilling and so personal, of suddenly seeing old manuscripts glow with new colors—of watching them magically become, in truth, illuminated manuscripts? Such was my fascinating experience—until, swept away by enthusiasm, I lost all sense of that proper shame which should possess one who searches out the private secrets of others—and sat down to write the Apostles all about themselves. I had found them out—and could not resist telling them so. As yet, they haven't "answered back" (but when that time comes, dear Reader, I shall crave your prayers!)

Of them, I shall also plead tolerance for these, my impertinences—which I shall explain were further nourished by an overpowering suspicion that has long possessed me. For I have suspected the Apostles (being in the first instance as human as you or I, though in the second instance holier than we can ever hope to be) of sometimes growing awfully tired of their remote relegation to cold, distant pedestals. I've wondered if occasionally they have not found their stiff, marble robes uncomfortable; and whether they have not sometimes deplored what is certainly none of their doing—their frequently unforgivably-tinted plaster garments. I've even speculated on the possibility that they just might, now and then, like to remove their gilt haloes for a bit—and make themselves at home with mankind. But mankind seems to prefer them to keep their formal distance; and is thus, I think, too often prone to regard them as strangers and not as the friends and brothers they actually are. With such an attitude, it is no wonder that as the centuries have rolled past since the Apostles dwelt upon earth, our faith in them has been *dimmed. For if we refuse to know personalities, how in truth can we believe in them?*

Do you not think anyway that man, generally, makes a ridiculous fuss over giving his faith to spiritual matters? Yet the strain put upon man to believe in God is nothing compared to the strain put upon God to believe in man. Of our credulence is asked so little—faith in Him, faith in His chosen Apostles, the miracles they wrought, His message which they taught. While we, on the other hand, expect Him to believe in the dignity of man as we nonchalantly go right ahead and stage, let us say, a world-war—and many other unpleasant things.

But now it's certainly high time that I draw this letter to a close. I submit herewith a copy of my correspondence with the Apostles. If you will be good enough to look it over, it is my timid hope that perhaps you and they may become better friends.

If that should happen, dear Reader—well, nothing in the world could make me really happier!

H. W. H.

CLEVELAND, OHIO.
FEAST OF SAINT SIMON AND SAINT JUDE,
OCTOBER 28, 1932.

CONTENTS

Foreword   v

I Love Saint Peter   3

My Apologies to Saint John   23

Please Take Me Fishing, Saint James   41

You Liked Parties, Saint Matthew!   57

Were You a Match-Maker, Saint Andrew?   73

Never Mind Them, Saint Thomas   95

The Ladies Liked You, Saint Philip   115

Without Guile, But Not Without Style,
      Saint Bartholomew!   135

In Justice to Saint James the Just   155

Were You Brothers, Saint Simon and Saint Jude? 175

To Saint Mark—Concerning the Purse-Bearer   191

An Epistle to Saint Paul   211

P.S. to Saint Paul   227

Will You Take the Case, Doctor Saint Luke?   243

xi

"And these signs shall follow them. ...In My Name they shall cast out devils: they shall speak with new tongues. They shall take up serpents; and if they shall drink any deadly thing, it shall not hurt them: they shall lay their hands upon the sick, and they shall recover."

— MARK ; XVI, 17

I LOVE SAINT PETER

I LOVE SAINT PETER

ALTHOUGH it may embarrass you greatly, Saint Peter, I cannot restrain myself any longer. I must confess I love you! Now, millions have always been dying to meet you; yet when it comes my turn, that will be true of me in a twofold sense. For though I only know you now as one upon whom I have pondered much, it will be like meeting a very old and very dear friend. And this is not meant as a subversive bid for your leniency toward my credentials, when that hour shall come—I hasten to tell you that, Saint Peter—though I have to admit it might be, if I thought it would do me any good. Those poor things—*eh bien, parlons d'autres choses*. It's far pleasanter to talk about you, Saint Peter!

I first began to love you when I had long curls and freckles and a propensity to mispronounce all strange and lengthy words that fell upon mine ear. Particularly did those I heard in Bible-class fascinate me. It was at this serious stage and age that you came into my life. Then, as your history was unfolded, my eager ears drew in every word of it. From the first, I loved you madly. I think it was because I felt so sorry for you. Insanely jealous was I for your sake, of Saint John—because John, we were told, was the Beloved Disciple—and I longed for an opportunity of explaining to Our Lord what a really fine man you were, Saint Peter.

When it was related to the little class how you had gone out and wept bitterly in penitence for the terrible denial—and how legend had it that you continued to weep so all the days of your life, the course of the tears leaving definite marks on your dear face—I, too, wept. Between sobs, I went home and explained that Saint Peter had wept until he had "two little gutters running down each side of his face." "Furrows," my precise mother corrected. Whenever reference was made to you in the Gospel on Sundays, I exulted —I took a personal pride in you—and if no mention was made of you, I sulked.

Nor shall you retort that my love was a mere childish fancy. Not at all—for even now, as I am passing into the sere and yellow, you are still, of all the Apostles, nearest my heart—and I love you just as dearly, if not as intelligently, as I did at seven.

To the theologians let it remain to expatiate on the high sanctity which shines so benignly down upon the world from your beautiful halo, Saint Peter. My own present, inconsequential concern in this letter is with your humanness. Please don't think me a bit odd, for all mankind, whether believer or agnostic, must be charmed— or so it seems to me—by this quality in you. The error of human frailty was not unknown to you— and I hope you are not going to take it amiss, when I say that in this respect if in no other I am very like you! How well I understand, for instance, that wonderfully wistful, somehow pathetic question you formed: "Lord, how often shall I forgive my brother? Till seven times?" Seven seemed *plenty*, didn't it, Peter? And then that little matter of falling asleep over your prayers. Alas, that I too—but never mind, we're discussing your shortcomings now. You'll have a chance to discuss mine later.

Among others of yours is reckoned the perfectly regardless way you had with you when handling a sword. I refer to that tragically dramatic moment when, the Last Supper completed, He led you all into the Garden of Olives, and Judas and "a band of soldiers and servants from the chief priests and the Pharisees, cometh thither with lanterns and torches and weapons." You were not going to let them seize your Master without putting up a fight; so, Saint John

5.

relates, "Simon Peter, having a sword, drew it, and struck the servant of the high priest, and cut off his right ear. And the name of the servant was Malchus." I know it's dreadful of me, but whenever I've read that passage, I've always whispered, "Good for you, Saint Peter!" So I deserve the rebuke your Gentle Master then voiced, every bit as much as you. Yet well do I understand how you felt! For ears can be such particularly obnoxious features—and to slice at them, at times, well nigh irresistible. I'm sure that Malchus's were of the unpleasant, protuberant variety, flapping back and forth in the breeze and listening to things it was no business of theirs to hear. But, after all, I'm sure you were relieved when your Lord restored that ear, unworthy as it was.

Superbly impervious were you, while on earth, to getting your feet wet—though all prudent people will tell you that such is the height of folly. Twice you are said to have behaved thus recklessly. You cannot have forgotten, Saint Peter, although it happened so long ago, that time when He had sent you and the others into your boat, to "go before Him over the water." Night had fallen, and you were having a difficult time managing the craft, "for the wind was contrary," when He came to you, "walking upon the sea." As soon as you were sure it was your Master, you simply couldn't wait until He reached the ship. Out you boldly sprang yourself upon the water and hastened to meet Him. It's a wonder you didn't catch pneumonia! As for me, I'm delighted that the Gospel doesn't say: "And Peter, seeing Who it was, stooped down, put on his galoshes, and stepped gingerly out upon the water."

And surely you still remember that other time, when you and six other Apostles had gathered by the Sea of Tiberias. Even though convinced of His Resurrection, you were a very mournful little band, missing woefully the comfort of His earthly presence. I've always thought, Saint Peter, that you heaved a prodigious sigh as you said to the others: "I go a-fishing." It was as though you sought this diversion to distract you, if possible, from the pain of that terrible sense of loss. You had loved Him so well. So, "I go a-fishing," you sighed. The others jumped at the suggestion. "We also come with thee," they announced. It is related that you remained on the water all night; though you caught nothing, for your heart wasn't in your work. But when dawn came softly, there, scarce two hundred cubits away, He stood upon the shore. Now, I can't help feeling a little sensitive because Saint John recognized Him first, Saint Peter (perhaps

7

his eyesight was a little better than yours); but, in any case, the minute you heard it was your Master, you again displayed the same old heedlessness. "Simon Peter ... girt his coat about him ... and cast himself into the sea." The boat wasn't half quick enough for you. What did you care about getting your cloak all wet? Now, Saint Bartholomew, also present, and always, I think, a little fussy about his clothes, didn't do any such crazy thing; nor, in fact, did any of them. For "the other disciples came in the ship." But, dripping as you were, I'm sure your Lord was very glad to greet you first.

Too, I've always sympathized with you for not being quite so fleet of foot as you might have been (I've no prowess myself in athletics). You may not like to be reminded, but there was that occasion when you ran a race with Saint John. It was the day following the Sabbath after your Lord's burial, and Mary Magdalen had hastened breathlessly into the room where you and Saint John were sorrowing, with the news that the Sepulchre was empty. Like a flash you were both on your feet, and racing to verify these amazing tidings. The record has it that John outran you (were you, perchance, a bit overweight?) and that you came in a puffing second. Nevertheless, though beaten, you contrived to be the first to enter into the Sepulchre. I so admire you for that, Saint Peter, though it baffles me to understand quite how you were able to accomplish it! One day I shall ask you to tell me.

In fact, there is a very great deal I long to ask you, for it seems that I can never learn enough about you, Saint Peter, even though the Gospels have more to say of you than of any other Apostle. But of your childhood, for instance, I only know that you were born in Bethsaida on Lake Genesareth, the son of Jona—and that you were really called Simon, up until that wonderful day when, a grown man, you were led by your younger brother, Saint Andrew, to the Master. He, looking upon you, said: "Thou shalt be called Cephas." "Which," continues Saint John, "is interpreted, Peter." Of course, I also know that you and your brother were fishermen in partnership with Saint James and Saint John. It is pleasant to think that you must have been successful, for you owned your own house in Capharnaum, where you were living at the time your Lord called you—and you also owned your own boat.

I love to picture that little house whose windows must have faced the sea—and to reflect especially upon that time when your Lord paid you the great honor of visiting it. You, always so hospitable, were never one to welcome only the

Choicest Guest and turn a cold shoulder toward others—for it is related that on that occasion you also invited your partners, Saint James and Saint John. I've always felt certain that, had the other Apostles been handy at the time, you would have included them all—no matter how limited the space and the silverware. Yet you could so easily have excused yourself from entertaining any but the Master, by saying truthfully: "I'd really love to have you all but, unfortunately, my mother-in-law is very ill!" Not you. Instead, you got round this difficulty by seeking the quickest means of curing her—in which you were most successful. For your Lord "lifted her up, taking her by the hand; and immediately the fever left her, and she ministered unto them." And, "when it was evening," we are told, ". . . all the city was gathered together at the door . . . and they brought to Him all that were ill." I'm sure you didn't mind a bit if these importunates trampled down your petunias—you were so over-joyed to see your Lord relieve their sufferings.

Now of course, Saint Peter, it goes without saying that, since you had a mother-in-law, you must have been married. (I do hope your wife doesn't object to your receiving odd letters from strange females!) Secretly, I've often wondered how she felt when she first heard how the Master, walking by the Sea of Galilee, where you and Andrew were casting a net, had said to you: "Come ye after Me, and I will make you to be fishers of men." That was all very well, she may have thought to herself, but if you were to give up fishing for fish, what was to become of her? Still, when she soon saw the love and trust the Master placed in you, and how you became the leader among all His followers, she must have been reconciled. And when she heard how He had said to you: "Thou art Peter, and upon this rock I will build My church, and the gates of hell shall not prevail against it; and whatsoever thou shalt bind upon earth it shall be bound also in Heaven; and whatsoever thou shalt loose on earth, it shall be loosed also in Heaven," she must indeed have been very proud of you! Her regrets over the fishing business—if she had any—could have been only temporary.

But I have a feeling that occasionally she must have had a difficult time holding you down, as it were—for I'm sure you were an extravagant soul. If she were at all practical or, rather, at all wifely, she must have been somewhat dismayed when she heard how, after He had been gloriously transfigured before you on that mountain-top, you had burst out with: "Let us make here three tabernacles; one for Thee, and one for Moses, and one for Elias!" She might have asked you, where was the money to come from? And wouldn't one tabernacle do just as well?

Which leads me on to the thought that maybe it was because you were a married man that you had acquired a certain deplorable tendency which, out of politeness, I shan't name. But perhaps you will guess what I mean, when I quote that passage which describes your behavior in the high priest's courtyard: "But Peter sat without ... another maid saw him, and she saith ... : 'This man also was with Jesus of Nazareth.' ... Then he began to curse and to swear that he knew not the man." If you get my meaning, don't take it too much to heart, Saint Peter. Everybody realizes that for years you'd had to live in the same house with your mother-in-law.

Yet no one was more conscious than you of your own failings. On that other time when you had been fishing all night and had caught nothing, and He commanded you to let down the net once more, and immediately you "enclosed a very great multitude of fishes," you fell at His feet, crying: "Depart from me, for I am a sinful man, O Lord!" But He knew you better than you knew yourself, and had no intention of ever departing from you. Though once He wondered if you would leave Him. "He that eateth this bread

12

shall live forever," was what He had been teaching; and "after this many of His disciples went back, and walked no more with Him. Then Jesus said to the Twelve: 'Will you also go away?'" The very suggestion appalled you. "Lord, to whom shall we go?" you demanded. "Thou hast the words of eternal life!" No half-way faith was yours. When, at the Last Supper, with basin and towel, He humbly approached you, you protested: "Thou shalt never wash my feet!" Yet, when He answered: "If I wash thee not, thou shalt have no part with Me," you cried: "Lord, not only my feet, but also my hands and my head!" You were in this thing up to your neck, and you intended to stick. No wonder, with all your little human frailties, He loved you so dearly, Saint Peter!

A very gifted thinker of our own day has declared that the time when He showed this love, this understanding, in its most human terms, was when He sent that message as you were suffering, after that most tragic Friday, in the upper room —grief-stricken at His death, heart-broken at your recent denial. For the angel at the Sepulchre had said specifically to Mary Magdalen: "Go, tell His disciples *and Peter*, that He goeth before you into Galilee; there you shall see Him, as He told you." Your Lord knew how you, particularly, were sorrowing; so you, of all His disciples, were to be especially singled out in that tender message of solace.

Of course He was certain of your love for Him, wanting you to show it in only one way, as He made quite clear that last time you plunged into the sea to meet Him. "Simon, son of John, lovest thou Me more than these?—Feed My lambs.—Simon, son of John, lovest thou Me?—Feed My lambs.—Simon, son of John, lovest thou Me?—Feed My sheep!" Confidentially, Saint Peter, I've always thought that the Syriac version of the New Testament recounts this episode much more charmingly than our own. For therein He is quoted: "Lovest thou Me?—Feed My rams.—Lovest thou Me?—Feed My sheep.—Lovest thou Me?—Feed My lambkins!" It seems most probable that the Good Shepherd was beseeching you to bestow His message equally upon men, women, and children, and that He thus classified them as rams, sheep, and lambkins. (It may be unworthy of me, but I can't help suspecting the otherwise upright translator of our own version of here indulging in a mild license simply because he couldn't bear himself to be categoried as a ram, with all its rambunctious implications.) And I'm certain that, wherever you preached, the lambkins especially clustered about you.

Thereafter you spent your entire life obeying these injunctions. You were indeed the Rock to which the others clung through all those first, perilous years; you led them all in boldness and in zeal. Truly upon you, and through you, was His church built as you fearlessly wrought signs and wonders in His name—curing the sick, and even bringing the dead to life. You were as heedless of the stripes and tortures your foes inflicted, as you had been, while He was with you, of getting a thorough soaking—and the prisons into which you were continually being popped, had a difficult time holding you. What did guards and locks avail, when you had His angels as accessories-after-the-fact? And no country was ever too distant or too difficult for you to evangelize. Into Galatia, Cappadocia, Bithynia, and Asia Minor, you carried His gospel through all those years—tirelessly, enthusiastically. But I think, Saint Peter, you must have particularly loved Rome, to which you journeyed as an old man— and Rome has certainly never forgotten you! Indeed how could she, when you so gloriously labored within her walls—and when finally Nero imprisoned and cruelly martyred you there? "When thou wast younger, thou didst gird thyself, and didst walk where thou wouldst. But when thou shalt be old, thou shalt stretch forth thy hands, and another shall gird thee, and lead thee whither thou wouldst not," the Master had long ago said to you. "And this," adds Saint John, "He said, signifying by what death He should glorify God."

I wish you would tell me if that charming legend concerning this period is founded on fact. I refer to the one which relates that during your incarceration your followers urged you to escape, and that even though you knew the time had at last come for you to lay down your life for Him, you humanly succumbed to their pleadings. It is said that you got as far as the city-gates, when suddenly you encountered your Lord entering them. Utterly taken aback, so the story goes, you inquired "Domine quo vadis?"—"Lord, whither goest Thou?" Sadly He replied: "I am come to Rome, to be crucified a second time." It is recounted that you needed no further hint, but immediately turned back and gave yourself up to the authorities. If all this really was so, Saint Peter, you more than made amends for that momentary faltering when your last hour approached. For we know that, when told you were to be crucified, you implored your executioners to reverse your cross, and to nail you upon it, head downward. You insisted you were not worthy to die as He had died—and they granted your plea.

Now is it any wonder that I love you, Saint

SAINT PETER

Peter? As when a child, so even today, when I see you on a stained-glass window, my sympathies are totally yours. For you are always laden with such a big, heavy bunch of keys. Don't you sometimes grow weary carrying them? And aren't you ever tempted to mislay them, and to utter the perfectly human excuse, "You see, I've lost my keys"? Being a fisherman, you would be pardoned for fibbing a little—and it must be such a dreary business, to be forever opening and shutting a door!

But there is still another matter which must be infinitely more irksome. I refer to the tedious and everlasting jokes about you which mankind has made down through all the Christian centuries, and to which you have had to listen, probably yawning your head off the while. What must you not have suffered for almost two thousand years by hearing: "The man died, and as he stood at the gates of heaven, Saint Peter said," etc., etc. And all the time you have been thinking, "When that one was first perpetrated, the infant King Arthur kicked the slats out of his cradle"— or words to that effect. I always feel like telling those jokers to beware! For even your patience may be tried too far. They should remember that to you belongs the last laugh—and he who laughs last—well, you know.

However, I dare to think that, tried though you have been, you will be indulgent in this matter. For of course you know the very fact that you, of all the Apostles, have been the most frequent subject of mankind's jokes, is only an added proof that you have been the most beloved! Whatever the worst that can be said of these jests, yet have they all been imbued with a spirit of affection—the kind one might make about a brother, for whom one's devotion is so sure that a little teasing only reaffirms it.

To you it was said: "Thou shalt catch men." You caught me long ago, Saint Peter. Even today, true to your old impetuosity, you are always bobbing up suddenly, when most needed. Not long ago, remote from all my daily and familiar haunts, I was walking, weary and depressed, and turned a sudden corner. Pop! There you were, standing on top of a nice old church, as comforting and kind and human as ever. I felt better at once. What did I care if generations of storms had made you a bit wobbly on your pedestal? Or that you were wearing your halo at a rakish angle? You were still my Saint Peter!

I often wonder if you really wore whiskers, as you are always depicted. I rather hope you did, for I even think that whiskers are human things—though there are some who would hold otherwise. If you did, I regret that I cannot also share these in common with you. However, there is yet another small something upon which I imagine we think exactly alike. "Again therefore Peter denied; and immediately the cock crew." —After that most tragic moment, all your life you must have shuddered when you heard one. Now, speaking for myself, I've always hated chickens and all barnyard fowl; and as for cock-crow—I simply detest it!

MY APOLOGIES TO
SAINT JOHN

MY APOLOGIES TO
SAINT JOHN

I REALLY owe you an apology, Saint John— you, the author of the beautiful Gospel— the writer of the Apocalypse and the three Epistles. But there have been others, too, who've owed you apologies, yet who've seldom had the grace to admit it. So I'm hoping that the very surprise of being asked will startle you into granting your pardon.

Think, before you refuse, of all those people who for centuries have busied their unpleasant selves in trying to prove that you never wrote your own Gospel. They've written libraries full of books, which in turn are full of arguments— as unconvincing as herds of centaurs in Central Park. Not that it's bothered you any. Nevertheless, apologies have certainly been due you—and there seem to be few instances where they've been rendered.

Even those authors who admit that you did write your own Gospel commit, with the above unattractive class, a certain wearisome gaucherie —though undoubtedly one that's well intended.

Nearly all of them throw Browning at your head. They quote at length from "A Death in the Desert." Now, you might be able to stand it once—but when it occurs repeatedly in dozens of books, it becomes a bit thick. Even Lord Charnwood quotes poetry about, and at you— you who wrote the greatest piece of poetical literature extant. Being a lord, he ought to have more *savoir-faire*.

Thus, before listing the affronts of which I've been guilty myself, it has seemed wise first to enumerate some of the glaring offenses of others, hoping that my very real sympathy might soften your mood before we reached the matter of my own delinquencies. Alas, they are indeed grave. First, it has taken me all these many long years really to appreciate you. And second, as I've already confessed elsewhere, I have been at times insanely jealous of you, for Saint Peter's sake. But the affair between Saint Peter and myself, one-sided though it be, is of such long standing, having arisen in my infancy, that perhaps you will forgive this jealousy—a natural emotion to green and unseasoned affection. I hope my love for Saint Peter is now more mature, and less susceptible to unworthy elements. If it isn't, I hasten to add that it's not his fault.

The lack of appreciation of you came, I

blush to admit, from never before having read the Apocalypse, nor your exquisite and self-illuminating epistles. Oh, yes—times without number had I been moved to the point of tears by the beauty of your Gospel.

"In the beginning was the Word, and the Word was with God, and the Word was God. . . . All things were made by Him: and without Him was made nothing that was made. . . . And the Light shineth in darkness, and the darkness did not comprehend It. . . . He was in the world, and the world was made by Him, and the world knew Him not. He came unto His own and His own received Him not. . . . And we saw His glory, the glory as it were of the only begotten of the Father, full of grace and truth."

When I would read this, I was satisfied that you were, indeed, the greatest of all the Apostles —but then I'd go away, and, "amid the cares of this world," forget for a little; and by and by begin to wonder about certain other matters concerning you. Then one day, not long ago, I found your letters to "The Lady Elect" (what a charming name to give your church!) and to Gaius. They changed everything—and my hitherto narrow horizon expanded into boundless beauty. But, to go back to those first reprehensible suspicions. It was my love for Saint Peter that made me bitterly resent the fact that in your Gospel, although you take pains to tell all about the poor man's denial of his Lord, you never mention a word about his repentance. All the other Evangelists carefully speak of his "going out, and weeping bitterly." If it hadn't been for this omission, I should have felt kindlier toward you from the beginning. And, in spite of my apologies, I hope some day to ask you—politely of course—for an explanation.

I also confess to a mean suspicion on discovering that you were the only one of the Evangelists to refer to yourself (if only by implication) as "that Disciple whom Jesus loved." All the others are strangely silent on that point. However, convinced at last that it wasn't just an idle boast, I now think the least Matthew, Mark and Luke could have done was to have paid you the courtesy of mentioning that fact also. And I don't blame you at all now. When you wrote your Gospel, many years after the Resurrection, you were the only one of the Twelve left—the last living person able to recount actual recollections of those wondrous days. If you had not left this record of the particular, special affection of the Redeemer for one of his friends, we should never have known that friendship, benign solace to all who must walk the rough way of life, had also greatly solaced

Him who trod the harshest way of all—the Way of the Cross. You followed Him to the end, and stayed near Him when all the rest had fled. You stood, looking up into His eyes as He died, having proved yourself worthy in those eyes of the last tender, beautiful trust He was to impose upon you. "When Jesus therefore had seen His Mother and the disciple standing whom He loved, He saith to His Mother: 'Woman, behold thy son.' After that, He saith to the disciple: 'Behold thy Mother.' And from that hour, the disciple took her to his own."—Now if my former point of view had not been so utterly biased, I should have realized from the start, that this trust alone (which even doubting critics admit you lovingly fulfilled through all the years up to the day when He called His Mother to Him) proves that you were, indeed, the "Beloved Disciple."

Aside from my first ignoble doubt on that matter, neither did I like the way in which you seemed to avoid any reference to the occasions on which you were really naughty and had to be rebuked. The other Evangelists are most specific on the subject of your shortcomings—but you admit nothing! It's perhaps not generous of me to remind you, but there was that time when the Samaritan village refused to give your Master shelter, and you, with your equally guilty brother, Saint James, begged for the privilege of calling down fire from Heaven to consume it. That was a nice, Christian wish, Saint John; and you received a proper scolding. One is happy to observe that it had an effect; for in later years you preached only love. Was it perhaps this bloodthirsty impulse of yours toward the unwary Samaritans that prompted your Master to call you and James, "Boanerges"—Sons of Thunder? Or was the name given you because you possessed powers of oratory? Or because of your deplorable tendency to call certain people "liars"? I hope you will tell me some day. It's a question that has puzzled me greatly.

We have Saint Mark's word for it that there was another occasion when you had to be put in your place. Seeing a man, not a follower of your Master, casting out devils in His name, you loftily forbade any such performance. The Gospel does not state,—but I very much hope you hastened back, after being reprimanded with the words: "He that is not against Me is for Me," and told the poor man he could go on with the good work.

On reading this item it also appears that just previously, as you were walking with the other Apostles to Capharnaum, you had all been indulging in an argument concerning which of you should be the greatest in the Kingdom He was to establish. You thought it was just a little private discussion among yourselves, and were rather startled when, on arrival, the Master asked you: "What did you treat of in the way?" Not one of you had the courage to own up—and you, like a small boy who had been into mischief, hastily endeavored to change the subject. Blushing, no doubt, you introduced the topic of forbidding that outsider to exorcise devils—I suspect you of thinking it would distract His attention, and even perhaps win you commendation! (It's not a cheerful thought to recollect how frequently I have acted likewise under somewhat similar circumstances, Saint John.) But your Master was not so easily diverted. Putting his arm about a little child, He said meaningly: "He that is the lesser among you all, he is the greater."

There is evidence, too, that you remained a "Son of Thunder" for some years after you grew older, and should have known better—for a story is current that one day you entered the baths and were very much annoyed to find cozily ensconced there, Cerinthus, the heretic, also moved by the desire to bathe. It is said that you rushed from the building, crying: "I fear to stay under the same roof with Cerinthus, lest it should fall in upon me!" Perhaps it's not for me to ask, Saint John—but was that any way to win over a heretic?

According to the records, the other Apostles were very much annoyed with you and your brother Saint James, because of your insatiable ambition at one time—but even in my most uncharitable moments, I never believed that you concocted that scheme of asking Our Lord for seats at His right and left hand. I prefer to accept Saint Matthew's account that it was your adoring, if misguided, mother who made the request. It would be quite like a mother—and leads to the suspicion that yours spoiled you, Saint John—for you were the youngest child, and she was well able to do so because your father, Zebedee, was a man of substance. We are told that he employed men in his fishing business to operate his several boats on the Sea of Galilee.

It appears that, no matter how much you might like to, you cannot put forth the same claim to democracy as can the other Apostles— for you even have to admit yourself, in your Gospel, that you were "known to the High Priest." We are led to assume that you were able to gain admission into his palace during your Lord's trial only because of this somewhat snobbish and unfair advantage. I'm glad, however, that you did come out and speak to the portress, assuring her that Saint Peter was "all right," and thus gaining him admission also. But I've often thought it was perhaps her disagreeable attitude before you spoke to her, which wore down his courage to such an extent that the poor man was driven, a few minutes later, into his lamentable denial. Like many of her terrifying profession, she probably demanded all sorts of social credentials from any who sought to enter those select precincts. As she let you pass without a question, the attitude of your own mother, Salome, in demanding the choicest seats in the "kingdom" for you and Saint James, becomes more understandable, if none the less rash—and since, later, Salome was among the holy women who followed Jesus and ministered unto Him—who stood at the cross at His death—and who went to the Sepulchre bringing sweet spices to anoint His body—it seems certain that she early won pardon from the Source of all forgiveness. But of course, she always "babied" you—and no doubt your colleagues did also, for in that circle, as in your family, you were the youngest of all.

I suppose, Saint John, that I really should have taken your youth into consideration, before judging so harshly your attitude toward that

Samaritan village, and the man casting out devils. Though, young as you were, you did not lack decision and courage—for when the Master called you from your father's boat, where you and Saint James were mending nets, you "forthwith left nets and father, and followed Him." It would indeed be a malicious person who might suggest that you had become a bit bored, mending nets—(still, and I'm only whispering it, Saint John, youth has always been notoriously reluctant to perform such family chores. In our own day, for instance, younger sons find cutting the grass a dull pastime).

Further careful analysis of your claim to being the "Beloved Disciple" discloses that you were certainly among the three most favored. It was "Peter and James and John" who were always selected from the rest to witness the greatest and most private events—the Transfiguration, the Agony in the Garden, and the raising of Jairus's daughter. And it was you and Saint Peter whom the Master sent ahead into Jerusalem, to make arrangements for the Last Supper. "Having loved His own," you gently tell us, "He loved them unto the end"—and you, sitting close to Him at that final repast, were permitted to receive a very special and beautiful token of that love.

Of the happenings that were to follow closely, Saint Mark recounts one in which many believe you were the chief actor. The ugly band sent by the chief priests to the Garden of Olives had seized your Lord, and "His disciples, leaving Him, all fled away. But a certain man followed Him, having a linen cloth cast about his naked body, and they laid hold on him. But he, casting off the linen cloth, fled from them naked." Somehow, you seemed to be always running—and very well, at that—as is evidenced from the race which you ran with Saint Peter, to see if, as had been reported that first Easter morning, the Sepulchre was really empty. You easily out-distanced him —but, as you were so much younger, I've never thought it was a victory of which you should boast. Even in my most relentless moods, however, I've had to admit that you were the first of the Apostles to believe that He had truly risen —and the first to recognize Him later from the boat, as He stood waiting for all of you on the shores of Tiberias. The gladness of your glorious cry rang out over the waters, its echoes never to die: "It is the Lord!"

Also, I've always rejoiced to think of you laboring so valiantly with Saint Peter in founding the early church—and of how your combined prayers healed that poor cripple at the Temple gate. But in my early and more savage years, when I read how this admirable coöperation with Peter once resulted in your both being thrown into prison, instead of a proper regret for your own predicament, I'm afraid I felt a little pleased —as long as Saint Peter had to be incarcerated, I did not want him to suffer alone!

When I realize what a charming old man you grew to be, I'm so ashamed of my early prejudices, Saint John. There is that lovely story told by Eusebius, which relates that you, converting a likely young man, went on your journeys, leaving him in the charge of one of your bishops. Returning to that church some time later, you missed him, and were not to be put off by the bishop's evasions:

"He is dead," said the bishop, briefly.

"How dead?" you firmly demanded.

"Dead to God," reluctantly admitted the bishop.

On pressing for details, you learned that the young man had fallen into evil ways, and thus into trouble with the authorities—and had fled to the mountains, where he had become the chief of a notorious band of brigands. You weren't going to allow anything like *that* to happen to one of your converts—and heedless to protests and fears for your safety, you set out for the bandit lair. You got yourself captured and brought before the murderous chief, who, when he saw you, did a surprising thing. He actually turned tail and ran away as fast as he could! But you, still adept as a sprinter, ran after the poor, terrified brigand and captured him—in more ways than one, for he returned with you, weeping, to the good life. You would be such a help to us in these lawless days, Saint John, if only we had you here!

You will remember that in recounting the last appearance of your Risen Lord on the shores of Tiberias, you wrote that Saint Peter, indicating you, inquired of Him: " 'Lord, and what shall this man do?' Jesus saith to him: 'So I will have him to remain till I come, what is it to thee?' This saying therefore went abroad among the brethren, that that disciple should not die." And indeed, Saint John, it certainly seemed for a great many years, as though you never would! For Tertullian relates that in Nero's reign you were taken to Rome and cast into a cauldron of boiling oil—from which you emerged, to the amazement of all, fresh as a daisy and quite unscathed. It is also recounted that you were forced to drink a cup of wine full of deadly poison which proved equally ineffectual. It must have been when they found they could not kill you that they exiled you to the Island of Patmos, where you received that glorious revelation of the Apocalypse. But surely you went with a peaceful heart —knowing that you had already sown the good seed in so many places—Ephesus, Smyrna, Pergamos, Thyatira, Sardis, Philadelphia, and Laodicea.

I love to think of you when, a very old man, too feeble to preach any longer, you would have yourself carried into the churches, only in order to say one thing to your flock: "Little children, love one another." Do you recall that someone once objected to this repetition which you had made so familiar, protesting: "Please, won't you vary the sermon a bit?" Isn't it strange that there are always people like that in every congregation, Saint John? But instead of being annoyed, you only remarked gently: "It is the Lord's command. If we fulfill it, we fulfill all things."

Somewhere it is charmingly recounted that you had a tame partridge which you deeply loved. I'm so glad you had, Saint John; for partridges are, I think, delightful; and you really needed a pet. You must have been very lonely in those last years. All on earth whom you had especially loved, had gone—your companions of the great adventure; the Mother of your Lord; and James, your brother, who had died a martyr's death. So I like to think of the partridge perching on your shoulder when you were writing those beautiful epistles. A venerable old man, you had come to think and write increasingly of love—though still remaining enough of a "Son of Thunder" to call a liar his plain name to his face! You began your letters by dubbing yourself "The Ancient"—you who had been a stripling when first you heard the lessons you were passing on in those missives. There is a lovely gentleness in the way you address "The Lady Elect," exhorting her with such endearments as "My Dearest," and imploring her to understand love. "In this we have known the charity of God, because He hath laid down His life for us; and we ought to lay down our lives for the brethren.... My little children, let us not love in word nor in tongue, but in deed and in truth.... For this is the charity of God, that we keep His commandments; and His commandments are not heavy." It is evident that you, Saint John, through your comprehension of love, had found them not only not heavy—but light and full of sweetness.

So you could write in the Apocalypse those beautiful words of solace: "...Death shall be no more, nor mourning nor crying, nor sorrow ...God shall dwell with men...and God shall wipe away all tears from their eyes."

Dear Saint John, when I read these things, more than ever do I know that I owe you multitudinous apologies. Please try to forgive me, for I have made a full and frank confession—and you must admit that it hasn't put me in a very good light. I've come to be really devoted to you, and I wanted you to know.

And if you happen to be seeing Saint Peter soon, will you please give him my love?

PLEASE TAKE ME FISHING, SAINT JAMES

PLEASE TAKE ME FISHING,
SAINT JAMES

IT may strike you as the oddest of requests, but I simply cannot refrain from asking you to take me fishing, Saint James. And I am addressing you, the Apostle known among the Jameses as "the Greater," and the older brother of Saint John. This detail, just to prevent you from doing what you might well feel inclined to do on receiving such a plea—mark it "Opened by mistake," and pass it on to Saint James the son of Alpheus, let us say. No, you don't get out of it as easily as all that. Now I know you have been asked to do many strange things in your day by prayerful petitioners all over the world, through all the Christian centuries, and I don't doubt that this is among the strangest. But for that very reason, I am hoping you will at least listen and hear me out.

It comes about in this wise. When I first began to read about you wonderful three, Peter and James and John, whom the Master so signally honored among the Twelve, selecting only you to witness all the most sacred events which befell during His ministry, it kept cropping up continually that you were fishermen. There you were in the first place, you and Saint John in your father's boat, mending your nets close to where Peter and Andrew were casting theirs into the sea, when the first marked honor came to you —the Master's voice calling you to follow Him. So much of the succeeding great adventure was spun about those fishing-boats and the blue waters of the Sea of Galilee which they rode so sturdily—and even the fish thronging its depths. Like Izaak Walton, I have always resented it when people speak disparagingly of these water-creatures, for they, humble as they are, were also honored by Him. Did He not multiply them on two occasions, to feed the hungry multitude; and did He not bid Peter draw a stater from the mouth of one, to pay the didrachmas; and did He not fill the nets to overflowing with them in a miraculous draught; and did He not even, when He appeared to the frightened eleven after His Resurrection, partake of one with honey, to show it was He in truth and not a spirit? Indeed, so often are fish and fishermen mentioned throughout the New Testament that it would almost seem as though every day had been a Friday. And you and Saint Peter and Saint John were the leaders in piscatorial pursuits; but you especially (or so I have reasoned it out) were the most skilled fisherman of the three.

Many will disagree with me, and claim that Saint Peter was—but then they will be thinking of him in his capacity as "fisher of men"; but when it came to being a fisher of fish, much as I like to see Saint Peter a leader in everything, I must admit it's probable that you far surpassed him and your brother. The reason is obvious. You were the most silent of the three. Haven't all piscatorial experts in all ages agreed that proficiency in the art is largely gauged by the ability to hold one's tongue? Now Saint Peter, the soul of impetuosity, seems to have been fairly talkative—indeed, the Gospels have him uttering more than a mouthful on many an occasion. No matter what the circumstances, he, at least, always had something to say. And while Saint John does not seem to have been nearly so loquacious, he, too, on occasion, could speak his mind; and as he was a prolific writer (to which his Gospel, his Apocalypse, and his three Epistles bear testimony) it is safe to infer that, like all writers, he did not have to be coaxed to talk. But you, present at all those astounding events most certainly evocative of comment, remained conspicuously silent. You left no writings behind you; the Epistle bearing the name of James came from the pen of the son of Alpheus. It would appear that you, of all men, knew how to keep your mouth closed. In that partnership—that fishing business—in which you and Saint Peter and Saint John were actively engaged until He called you, much of the material success I'm sure was due to you, the silent partner.

Others again may disagree with me about your natural reticence, on the score of the title you shared with your brother—"Sons of Thunder." But since I wrote a certain apology to Saint John and referred to the reason for this appellation, a different and more convincing light has dawned. No longer do I speculate upon the possibility of the name having been given you because you could thunder so eloquently from those early Christian pulpits. It rather seems probable that calling you "Sons of Thunder" was simply another way of calling you "Sons of Zebedee." For your father Zebedee, I take it, was a man of some temper. Certainly, Saint John inherited a temper (which he learned beautifully to control) from someone. Saint Mark relates that when the Master called you and your brother, immediately "leaving their father Zebedee in the ship with his hired men, they followed Him." Now Zebedee probably did not know at the time Who was thus annexing his two stalwart sons.

Yet you left him flat, with double the work to do. Of a certainty, he must have thundered at you to come back. Even a father without a temper might have been excused for doing so. It is likely that Zebedee's lusty protestations were still ringing in the Master's ears when he christened you two "Sons of Thunder."

As for the inference that you had a thunderous disposition yourself, which might be drawn from that pleasant little suggestion of calling down fire from Heaven to destroy the churlish Samaritan village, I suspect Saint John of really conceiving that scheme. For although he was your younger brother, undoubtedly he was the leader in all the activities (except fishing) which you pursued together. It is recounted that he had found and recognized the Master even before that memorable day on which He called you both; and many writers have assumed that his enthusiasm and faith, poured forth as he related his portentous discovery to you, were the motivating forces in your own willingness to follow your Lord. This younger brother really got you started—just as Saint Peter's younger brother got him started, it being Andrew who, of that pair, first found the Messiah.

At least to my satisfaction, then, a man of silence, is it any wonder I'm sure you could teach me more about fishing than any of them? This, in spite of a disquieting inner voice which asks me if I think even a great saint could teach me how to keep quiet. Well, if anybody could, perhaps you could, Saint James—so let us leave it at that. Indeed, I should love to go fishing with you. Now there are lots of other things I'd like to do with Saint Peter, such as—but I'd best take those up with him personally.

Not only were you silent, but one might also suspect you of being somewhat inert during His ministry. Yet it should be plain to anyone why you were. You were simply "saving up"—for, in the end, you were to be so gloriously active. If you didn't do much during your Master's life other than look on, a privileged witness, at the restoration to life of the little daughter of Jairus, at the Transfiguration and at the Agony in the Garden, you were to make up for it later by outstripping all the other Apostles in being the first to die for your Lord. And if you weren't very active during your life, you were certainly singularly busy after your death—for you are reported to have miraculously appeared no less than thirty-eight times!

You really must have been a delightful person, Saint James—quiet and comforting, unexcitable, serene and dependable; with little to say, but thinking deeply on all the wondrous things that befell that company—silently storing away the impressions that were to build up within you a faith so firm that it enabled you to meet martyrdom magnificently; setting the first glorious example to the others who must follow you along that cruel path of blood. Let them (no doubt you thought to yourself) be leaders in life—you would lead them all in death.

Some would accuse you of being quite a sleepy-head—for you are reported to have fallen asleep on two occasions when you really should have been very wide awake—on the crest of that high mountain where you were led to witness the Transfiguration, and in the Garden of Olives when He took you aside to pray. But so also did the other two of that favored trio—so I don't think it's nice to throw it up only to you.

You could tell me, if you would, Saint James, whether tradition is correct in claiming that when the Apostles set forth to "teach all nations," you went to Spain, to whose people you preached the Gospel. It is said, too, that on this mission you were accompanied by Abenadar— no less a person than that centurion who, at the Crucifixion, had been stationed at the foot of the cross, and who, when the heavens darkened and the earth shook, had cried: "Indeed, this was the Son of God!" We are told how, there in Spain, you grew to love the people you had come to teach—and how, though at length you had to go back to Jerusalem, it was with the fixed hope of one day returning to their sunny, kindly land. It is believed that you did, indeed, return; but not in life, for even as you bade those shores farewell, death was lying in wait for you in Jerusalem within the marble walls of the palace of Herod Agrippa.

The events which followed were to prove that, slow of speech though you may have been, whatever you did say, you meant. Fourteen long years before had occurred the almost unique occasion when you are credited with speaking. It was right after your mother Salome had committed the rash indiscretion of asking the Master to give you and your brother, Saint John, the choicest seats in the Kingdom. Your Lord had asked you both: "Can you drink of the chalice that I drink of, or be baptized with the baptism wherewith I am baptized?" Staunchly you had answered Him: "We can." After your return from Spain, you alone were called upon to prove that assertion, and you neither quailed nor faltered. "And Herod, the king, stretched forth his hand to afflict some of the Church. And he killed James, the brother of John, with the sword." As fully as was possible, you drained the chalice which He had drunk, not forgetting that, with its last dregs, He had forgiven His enemies. For Eusebius has a story, culled from a lost writing of Clement of Alexandria, which recounts that one Josias, a prominent Pharisee, went by night to Herod and betrayed you to him as a leader in the sect the king sought to exterminate. At your trial, Josias was present; but the beauty of your fortitude and faith completely won him. He became a Christian. The indignant Herod also condemned him to death, and together you were led to the executioner. Just before the sword descended, Josias begged of you complete forgiveness for his betrayal unto death, and you, uttering a gentle "pax vobiscum," kissed him tenderly on both cheeks. Thus you died. And thereafter began your really active life.

Certainly, after your death, you and Spain were tremendously occupied with each other. An old codex of the Monks of Marchia relates that, after your martyrdom, Hermogenes and Philetus, with other of your disciples, carried your body to the seashore, where they were delighted to find a splendid, seaworthy ship, miraculously there for their purpose. On it they placed your mortal remains and set sail; but soon all were overcome by sleep. They awoke one morning to find themselves, surprisingly, off the coast of Spain—in fact at Padron (the ancient "Iria Flavia") itself, where you had preached the Gospel. There, chanting the while "In mare viae tuae et semitae tuae in aquis multis" ("Thy way is in the sea, and thy path in the great waters"), they carried your body ashore and laid it upon a great stone. The various legends, differing in minor points, all agree as to what immediately followed. The hospitable stone at once opened its arms to receive you, and then protectingly covered you. Right under your disciples' astonished noses, you were sheltered in a nice, stone tomb—and they were saved the trouble of laboriously hewing one out of the rock.

Other accounts would have it that, dead though you were on that seafaring journey, you didn't need any help at all from your disciples. They affirm that you sailed all by yourself in a ship from Joppa to Spain, and that the vessel was a wonderful thing, scorning the use of sails, propelled by angels, and fashioned of the costliest marble. I'm sure that if you did choose to travel in this manner, Saint James, it would have been easy for you—only I do hate to give up the disciples' chant of that lovely Latin song. So I rather hope you didn't make the journey *tout seul*. However it was, once you were safely

encased in that friendly stone, you were not allowed to rest there long—for the pagan Queen
Lupa heard of the veneration which quickly cen-
tered about it, and gave orders for its immediate
destruction. She commanded that it be harnessed
to wild bulls (they didn't let you forget you were
in Spain!) and violently dragged about until it
fell to pieces. Your terrified disciples, eyeing the
foaming, rearing animals, quickly made the sign
of the cross over them, and they at once became
mild as doves. With the utmost docility, they
gently dragged you, stone and all, right up into
the royal court-yard—thus converting to Christianity Queen Lupa and all her domain.

But in the dark ages soon to overshadow
Spain, when she lay under the yoke of the Mos-
lems, you were sadly neglected—and finally no
one even remembered where you were buried.
It was only in the year 835 that you were found
and honored again. Then, it is related, Theodo-
mir, Bishop of Iria, investigated rumors that
strange, beautiful lights had been seen to glow
over a certain thickly wooded copse, and that
there an angel had appeared. Within the copse
he found your tomb. He related his discovery
to King Alfonso the Chaste, who at once, with
great reverence, removed you to Compostella,
and there established a see. Then began the great

veneration for you which made your shrine perhaps the most popular of all the places of pilgrimage throughout the middle ages, and which led to the founding of the order of Santo Jago—Santiago da Compostella, as we know it.

An unknown French monk who, toward the beginning of the twelfth century, wrote "Le Livre de St. Jacques," recounted therein a different version of the finding of your body after Spain had so shockingly mislaid it. He claimed it was actually Charlemagne who discovered it (being a Frenchman, he *would*) and who one night saw a dazzling pathway of stars spanning the sky, and ending directly above the spot where you lay. He also said that you appeared to the French emperor, and ordered him to make war on the Saracens. If you really did this, Saint James, I'm sure Saint John put you up to it—but I'm rather inclined to think you never did; and that Charlemagne made up the story as the best excuse he could think of at the time for one of his long campaigns—propaganda for the pacifists of his day.

Far more in character is the legend of the emblem which always distinguished you in mediaeval art—the scallop shell. This, with the pilgrim's staff and cloak, served to identify you. Now some prosaic and earthy-minded folk have claimed that the scallop shell stood only for the dish from which you, as a pilgrim, ate your food—but those who really know you best affirm that it became your mark in the following fashion. When the miraculous ship was bearing you to Spain, it passed close to the shores of Portugal. There on the beach disported a merry company. A bridegroom and his friends were galloping their horses along the sands as they waited for the nuptial hour to strike. To the horror of all, the bridegroom's powerful mount became unruly, and suddenly plunged into the sea. He and his rider were making for a watery grave when you obligingly changed the course of your ship, and headed him back to land—thus delivering from death a dripping and badly frightened bridegroom. Shivering as he was, he at once ascertained the nature of the ship that had saved him, and not even stopping to change, became a Christian. His garments, which were at once his baptismal and wedding robes, were encrusted with scallop shells, which had attached themselves to him in his watery plunge. From this story might we not also argue that you rather believed in encouraging matrimony?

Be all this as it may, Saint James, it is not at all strange to me that you surrounded yourself with scallop shells. It's only natural that with your gift for fishing, you should have an affection for scallops. For the dictionary defines them as "marine, bivalve fish." Perhaps, even, we might find a few—if you would only take me fishing, Saint James!

YOU LIKED PARTIES,
SAINT MATTHEW!

YOU LIKED PARTIES,
SAINT MATTHEW!

I'M so glad you liked parties, Saint Matthew. For I like them very much myself. When frequently others have deplored my enthusiasm for them, I've always been able to silence their protests by remarking: "Even Saint Matthew was fond of throwing a little party now and then." I hope you don't mind. It really has been one of the thoughts that has brought me closest to you. It's evident you had a weakness for parties because you are the only one of the Twelve ever recorded to have given one. Now, as you'll agree, Saint Matthew, many people like parties well enough to go to them—but not so many like them well enough to give them. You do have to like them tremendously for that.

When I remind you that you were the only one of the Twelve ever to give a party, I'm not forgetting for a moment the warm hospitality of Saint Peter, for instance, who was always eager to fling wide the doors of his house in Capharnaum to all who wanted shelter. Among you Apostles, he was, of course, the soul of hospitality; just as was, among the Disciples, Saint Philip. For I've heard that Saint Paul frequently visited in the latter's home—in spite of the four prophetic daughters his host is said to have had. But hospitality and the taste for parties *per se*, are two different things; and while Saint Peter and Saint Philip enjoyed entertaining house-guests, there is no reference to their ever having given, as you did, a real party.

What with this, and other matters, I've been thinking a great deal about you lately, Saint Matthew—how, in that Roman-governed province of Judea where you lived, you were at first one of the native tax-gatherers appointed by its conquerors, to wrest every penny of taxes possible out of the hands of your fellow Jews. Of course it was a position which did not enhance your popularity with the latter. You were called a "publican" and I hope you'll forgive me, but for a long time I thought of you in the other sense of publican, feeling sure you had kept a tavern. But perhaps you would have preferred such an occupation to your own, for certainly much disrepute clung to your profession. Your class was accused, not only of being unpatriotic Jews for holding office under the despised conquerors, but also because of your contact with these Gentiles, of being stigmatized with ritual uncleanliness. But I've often reflected how you had, in a worldly sense, at least one compensation for the social ostracism you suffered—and that was wealth. Your office was certainly a lucrative one; and after all, even if the Jews wouldn't come to your parties, you publicans could give lovely ones to each other. You had plenty of money for travel, and pleasure, and fine clothes—and wasn't it true that the social barrier didn't worry your class very much? Of course, Saint Matthew, originally you must have had a fondness for all these luxuries, or you would never have chosen your profession. And that's what makes your conversion one of the most interesting among the Twelve.

I like to think how you, even as those fishermen, Peter and John and their brothers, were busy at work when the great summons came—and how like them, you rose up unhesitatingly and followed Him. We know that you, at least, were leaving a very profitable business; and it must have been a most interesting one. For your office in Capharnaum was on the great road that ran by the Sea of Galilee—that road which was the main thoroughfare connecting such far-flung marts as those of Egypt and Damascus. Over it came, in splendid, colorful procession, the rich caravans of powerful merchants, who must have been interesting men to deal with—brave, adventurous, and full of tales of strange, foreign ways and lands. On the backs of their heavy-laden camels must have rested all manner of odd and beautiful things which it was their duty to uncover before you, and to pay whatever tax you saw fit to impose as the right of imperial Rome.

Many times I've pictured you, on that summer day in that particular year of the governorship of Herod Antipas, as you were busy at work. By virtue of your office, a certain percentage of all you levied was yours—and perhaps you may literally have been counting your shekels, when the greatest moment in your life came. "And when Jesus passed on from thence, He saw a man sitting in the custom-house, named Matthew; and He saith to him: 'Follow Me.'" Nothing mattered after that; you were ready to chuck the whole business—riches, costly apparel, worldly pleasures. All you asked was one final fling, by way of celebration—a party—a party in honor of Him! And no small measly party at that! The Master graciously accepted your invitation; and you determined that all His friends, as well as your own, should be invited. Since His companions were mostly humble fishermen, or men and women who up until recently

had been notorious sinners; and since yours included all the heartily despised publicans of the
neighborhood, it can't be said that "among
those present," were any names included in the
contemporary Social Register. On the contrary,
the motley and questionable group gathered
about your lavish board caused no end of
scandal. Saint Mark says that "many publicans
and sinners sat down together"; while Saint
Luke relates that you "made a great feast," in
your "own house; . . . but the Pharisees and
Scribes murmured, saying to His disciples: 'Why
do you eat . . . with publicans and sinners?'"

But anyway, I'm sure that you, Saint Matthew, a true lover of parties for themselves,
weren't in the least disturbed. You hadn't a snobbish bone in your body, nor the slightest ambition to appear in the society columns. A party
to you meant only a gathering about you of those
who were congenial, to whom it was your pleasure to serve the choicest viands and wine. In
your own Gospel, like a perfect host, you say
nothing about the sumptuousness of the feast—
yet with careful candor you do speak of the assembled "publicans and sinners." I feel certain
that you had a very good time at your own
party. I wonder if it was also the occasion when
the Master changed your name from Levi to

Matthew? Certain it is that before this you had been known as Levi. But He chose to call you Matthew, or, in Hebrew, *Mattai,* as it had been shortened from the original *Mattija*—a great compliment, since it signifies "Gift of Jehovah."

Barred though you may have been from what was considered decent society, it's nevertheless evident that you were a man of education. Your parents, Alpheus and Mary, must have been people of means, for you had been well trained in the knowledge of Jewish law and Scriptures, and no doubt had studied under one of the great rabbinical teachers. You certainly knew your Prophecies, as you were to demonstrate when you wrote your Gospel, in which you repeatedly proved their fulfillment in the life and death of your Master. It's plain also that you had a flair for genealogy—being able, with the utmost ease, to trace His descent back to Abraham. "The book of the generation of Jesus Christ, the son of David, the son of Abraham," you began your great work; and then proceeded to show how all this was. I like to think that He, knowing, although it was yet unwritten, what that Gospel would mean to the world, was considering all these things when He called you, "Gift of Jehovah."

There has been a difference of opinion as to whether it was you, or Saint Mark, who first wrote down a record of that Divine Ministry which was to be the original Gospel; but I'm sure, as much as it has been argued about down here below, that it has never been a matter for words between you and Saint Mark. You are not, either of you, that sort of author. It is, however, generally conceded that your work, written about six years after the Ascension, was first known as "The Oracles," or the sayings of Jesus. And I don't know how you feel about it, but I rather resent that passage from Papias, preserved by Eusebius, which states: "So then Matthew composed 'The Oracles' in the Hebrew language, and each one interpreted them as he could." Did he mean to imply anything against your lucidity? If he did, I wish you'd just call his attention to the rapidity with which you were translated into Greek, and widely circulated.

You seem to have been every bit as much a man of action as a man of letters. According to Saint Irenaeus, you were very busy after your Lord's death, preaching and founding churches throughout Judea; and Saint Clement of Alexandria states that you were so occupied for fifteen years. Nor did you go about all this quietly, as one fearing the persecution then smoldering and likely at any moment to break out into violence against all Christians. Not you! For Rufinus has you accepting the challenge of the high-priest to public debate; subject: the ancient Jewish rites of sacrifice, versus the new Christian rite of baptism. Standing on the Temple steps, boldly you faced all Jerusalem; and capably you knocked your opponent's arguments into a cocked hat. "Having made these and such like statements," continues Rufinus, "Matthew stopped." And that settled *that* debate.

But how much further afield were your labors eventually to carry you! Dorotheus and Paulinus both state that you preached the Gospel in Parthia; and Socrates, the fifth-century ecclesiastical historian, says: "When the Apostles divided the heathen world by lot among themselves, to Matthew was allotted Ethiopia." According to some of the Greek legends concerning this territory, I cannot think you were entirely lucky at matters of chance—for it was reputed to include a country known as Myrmidonia, peopled entirely by cannibals! Paradoxical, indeed, that a land possessing such a pretty poetical name, could espouse such unpleasant customs. Hearing "Myrmidonia" for the first time at that Apostolic lottery, you probably thought: "That sounds like a nice, idyllic place to visit." But when you got there, tradition has it that you were unpleasantly surprised. Your first sermon did indeed draw a crowd—but, awkwardly enough, their minds were not on spiritual matters. The Myrmidonians thumped you up and down, and finding you sound and plump, decided you would make an excellent meal. So they cast you, and your two disciples, Rufus and Alexander, into a dungeon, while they set about warming the oven and preparing the sauce. If it hadn't been for Saint Andrew, who happened along at the time and rescued you, you would certainly have been in a pretty stew. He neatly dispatched seven cannibal guards—you were released, and borne comfortably off, on a soft cloud, to a far-away mountain where, one surmises from the Apocrypha, you were eventually left completely alone.

How often I've thought of you there, as you undertook those solitary forty days of fasting and prayer! You who had once delighted in the costliest raiment, now only allowed yourself a tunic of the poorest material—and not so much as sandals for your poor feet. And I love that part of the story which recounts that as you were praying in this solitude, a beautiful little child suddenly stood beside you. Immediately that instinct of hospitality—what was left of the old urge to "give a party"—rose within you, for you exclaimed:

"And why, O Child highly favoured, hast thou come hither? Because here is a desert; and what sort of table I shall lay for thee, O Child, I know not; because I have no bread, nor oil in a jar.... Even the winds are at rest, so as not to cast down from the trees anything of food; because for the accomplishing of my fast of forty days, I, partaking only of the fruits falling by the movement of the winds, am glorifying my Jesus. Now, therefore, what shall I bring thee, beautiful boy? There is not even water near, that I may wash thy feet."

Poor Saint Matthew! You were indeed distressed, not to be able to entertain your guest more substantially. But quickly you were comforted; the little child revealed himself as your Lord. We are told that He gave you a rod, which He bade you take down the mountain and into— of all places!—the city of the man-eaters. Bravely swallowing your qualms, you obediently set forth. In view of your former experience at the hands of the Myrmidonians, it must have been slightly comforting to reflect upon your recently accomplished forty days' fast. You would not, in any case (you probably told yourself), seem quite such a tempting morsel as previously.

Nevertheless, you must have quaked as you drew near the city-gates; but distraction soon offered.

Weren't you relieved to be met there by Queen Fulvana and her son and daughter-in-law —even though all three were possessed by evil spirits? For it gave you a chance to forget your own troubles and to exorcise these devils—thus converting the royal trio. Then, it is related, you proceeded according to instructions to plant the rod, which immediately grew into a great and beautiful tree, with a fountain springing from its roots. I like to think of the Myrmidonians bathing, out of sheer curiosity, in these waters, and how the immersion at once miraculously converted them. But the King, bewildered and upset by your influence upon his wife (rid of her devil, she seemed so strange to him) ordered his man-eating subjects to gobble you up just as fast as they could. I rejoice that they, having now gone over to a nice Christian, vegetarian diet, refused. So the King, we are told, called upon that familiar old devil whom you had driven out of the Queen, but who was still skulking about— by name, one Asmodaeus. It must have been rather satisfying to you, to have the latter admit himself pretty well defeated—even though he did advise the royal husband to see if you couldn't be disposed of through fire. A great blaze was started on the seashore, and you were placed in its midst. But, as you recall, the fire would have none of you; and the indignant soldiers had to report to the King that you were as so much asbestos—and that your fellow Christians were having a grand time, running about, unscathed, in the flames, and actually laughing at them! Asmodaeus then attempted to conquer your power by circling the fire with the King's own great gold and silver idols, but they were melted to nothing by the blazing heat. Do you remember how the distracted monarch, practical even in such a moment, cried out: "Woe is me! Better are the gods of stone and earthenware, in that they are neither melted nor stolen!"?

There has been no end of argument as to whether the King of Myrmidonia finally got his bonfire to work, wherein you died a martyr's death; or whether you escaped, eventually to die a nice, cool death in bed as claimed by Heracleon. In any case, it is supposed that you left this earth about the year 90 A.D. Paulinus and Dorotheus state that you died in Hierapolis; and of those who claim you met a martyr's death, some maintain that it was inflicted by the sword. Only you can really enlighten us, Saint Matthew —for the Roman Martyrology merely says: "S. Matthaei, qui in Aethiopia praedicans martyrium passus est." The Greek Church calendar substantiates the Myrmidonian theory to the extent of crediting you with a fiery martyrdom; and certain legends claim that, when the King got you well burned, he had your coffin sealed with lead and thrown into the sea. Undismayed, you are said to have risen from the depths, coffin and all, set upon a cross, before the astonished eyes of His Majesty, who then became a Christian. What a stubborn old thing he had been, to be sure, Saint Matthew! For all will agree that you had already given him ample proof of the truth of Christianity, without his requiring of you this last remarkable feat.

Mingled as are fact and legend concerning you, Saint Matthew, one substantial conviction emerges—you were indeed (at least, after your publican and party days) the Gift of Jehovah. We owe you much. You were the only one of all the Evangelists to record the Sermon on the Mount in full—in all its Divine beauty and tender solace. Because you reported those words, uttered that long-ago day on Kurn Hattin, so fully and so carefully, they must have meant, out of all that multitude listening to Him, something special and significant to you.

"Blessed are the poor in spirit." (Were you, perhaps, thinking as He spoke, of that gold upon

which you had recently set such great store?)
"Blessed are the meek." (Was the pride you had
so lately felt in your vested authority, then in
your mind?) "Blessed are they that hunger and
thirst after justice." (Had you a lurking sorrow
that perhaps you had not always wielded your
power fairly?) "Blessed are the merciful." (Had
it been your duty to turn over to the authorities
those who could not pay their tax?) "Blessed are
the clean of heart." Dear Saint Matthew, the life
of renunciation, love, labor and prayer you lived
so gloriously, eventually made yours white as
snow; and you worthy indeed, at the end, to "see
God."

As for me, I must confess I think one of your
most heroic sacrifices (in view of your decided
flair for them) was your renunciation of parties.
Yet, after all, that is only a personal, and no
doubt unworthy, point of view.

WERE YOU A MATCH-MAKER, SAINT ANDREW?

WERE YOU A MATCH-MAKER,
SAINT ANDREW?

Now please don't misunderstand me, Saint Andrew, when I ask if you were a match-maker. For I'm not puzzling over whether or not you were a manufacturer of safety-matches. The matches to which I have reference are alleged by sceptics to contain no such element as safety— although that is a matter of opinion. Frankly, I mean, were you one to give a good shove to those timid souls hesitating on the awesome brink of matrimony?

As far as you yourself were concerned, one of the first called to leave all things and follow Him, I suspect that among those things was no wife. For we do know that at that time you were living in your brother's house at Capharnaum, enjoying what I would consider the most enchanting of privileges—of being a member of Saint Peter's own household! But very often it is those who refuse to make matches for themselves who evince the greatest enthusiasm in making them for others; so your own suspected bachelorhood offers no alibi. And while there is no Scriptural reference to your interest in *affaires-de-coeur*, tradition would make you, in matters romantic, quite as active as Saint Valentine himself. As you very well know, it has induced since the memory of man runneth not, Slavic, German, and Russian maidens to plead with you on the eve of your Feast to send them nice husbands. It would certainly seem that, if you hadn't been keenly interested in matchmaking, this custom would not have prevailed over so many centuries and in such a diversity of lands. Indeed, Saint Andrew, I would give anything to know just what you did while on earth to justify this faith in your ability to aid the lovelorn.

Surely those young people of Germany who, on the eve of the thirtieth of November, take pains to float tiny paper boats in water, invoking your name the while, have some justification for their custom. Each boat carries a boy's or girl's name, and it is believed that if you, Saint Andrew, direct two of the boats together, the two young people bearing those names shall wed. If you allow one to float away in solitary exclusiveness, it's a foregone conclusion that that name shall remain forever unmated. Then there are those romantic Russian maidens who even arise before dawn on your Feast-day; though I don't think their objective, the chicken-roost, is a particularly romantic place. Nor do I think they are quite fair to those hungry hens as the poor things, anticipating a feeding, cluck toward them. For each wily maiden, murmuring her prayers to you, heartlessly drops only a gold piece, a copper piece, and a pinch of ashes. Don't try to deny, Saint Andrew, that if you direct the fowl toward the gold, you are promising the maiden a rich husband; if toward the copper, a poor one; and if toward the ashes—well, she is to understand there will be no wedding at all, but rather, a funeral! It all must keep you terribly busy at the time of your Feast; and no doubt you are greatly relieved each year when the first of December dawns.

In these lovers' behests, I think the German young people are rather more tactful than the Russians. For they employ water and boats, both of which were greatly favored by you, who were preëminently a sailor—while the Russians use hens; and as I've often said, I for one can never believe that hens (or cocks, at least) are very popular in your family. That is, not if you're the loyal brother to Saint Peter you really should be.

In spite of all this, the Evangelists and the early Fathers, strangely enough, must have considered romantic matters of little moment—for they haven't left so much as a crumb of evidence linking you to lovers. Pages and pages have been written regarding your powers in other fields; and justly so, for you were indeed one of the greatest of the Apostles. You must truly have had the strongest of personalities, not to have been completely over-shadowed by that amazing brother of yours.

I love to think of you two fishermen, the sons of Jona, with those other brothers, your partners Saint James and Saint John, putting out together in a boat on the Sea of Galilee, all with high hopes of a fine catch. While I think it was Saint James who, of that partnership, had the greatest flair for fishing, I'm convinced that you, Saint Andrew, were the most skilled with boats. For you seemed to love all things pertaining to the water; in fact, you have the reputation of having, in your later life, sailed the seven seas themselves to spread the message of your Master before you at length laid down your life for Him. Of all the Apostolic parents, yours at least seemed to know what they were about when they named their child; for "Andrew," I've learned, signifies "Valor." The Master, when He called you, found no cause to rename you more suitably—as He did in the case of at least two of your companions.

He knew that throughout your long life you would be always, indeed, Andrew the Valorous. And although the Gospels make no mention of it, I am sure that on that time when the Apostles were sailing, and He slept in the boat, "and there came down a storm of wind ... and they were filled, and were in danger; and they came and awakened Him, saying: 'Master, we perish,'" that you at least were not frightened. We know that the sea held few terrors for you—else why should the Russian Royal Navy, as long as it existed, have proudly borne your cross upon its flag?

Of course you were, in fact, up until the Revolution, the patron-saint of all Russia; which was as it should be, for had you not once sailed up the river Dnieper and planted the Cross on the heights of Kiev? It distresses me that after so many centuries you should recently have been supplanted in that country. Although personally not at all responsible, I blush to remind you that they have set up in your place one Lenin. At least, publicly—and nicely done in ice, I understand. But as to what goes on privately, while in no position to speak with authority, I'm willing to wager a good many roubles that those lovelorn Russian maidens still continue to beseech you with the full certainty that you will listen to them far more sympathetically and effectively than will any Lenin!

Concerning Scotland, who also early chose you for her patron-saint, I've often wondered just where on earth she would ever be without you. Though with less reason than Russia (you are supposed to have actually visited the latter in person, but it is said you only sent your bones to Scotland—after your death, of course), yet has she been far more loyal. As all will agree, if the Scotch are anything, they are canny. They know a good thing when they've got it. Ever since that day in the year 761, when the monk Regulus, guided by a vision (or so runs the Chronicle of the Picts and Scots) landed on their rugged coast carrying your holy relics, the Scotch have never faltered. Whether it was really Regulus, or as some claim Saint Augustine, who first brought them your venerated bones, has not troubled them greatly. Suffice it that you early answered their prayers in battle, completely routing the foe —thenceforth your cross became their national banner. And from that day to this, as you know, practically every other male child in the country has been christened Andrew! You have certainly repaid their devotion in a thousand ways. Perhaps the one most appealing to this frivolous generation lies in what you have done for them since they named their first golf-links for you. They called it the Royal and Ancient Golf Club of Saint Andrew's—and you, not to be outdone, turned right around and made them the greatest golfers in the world! You are truly a sporting saint—with your devotion to sailing, and your sympathy for golf; to say nothing of your intrepid coöperation in your petitioners' love-affairs.

As splendid as all this is, Saint Andrew, I very much fear that as a child, you were really rather trying. Now, confidentially, isn't it true that you were one of the sort who perpetually ask questions? In spite of all your marked virtues, I can't help feeling a certain sympathy for your poor mother, who must have been forever hard put to it to answer all your queries. Between this intellectual strain and her efforts to keep you from venturing out upon the water in any sort of weather, I'm really forced to infer that there must have been more "comfortable," if less interesting children in the neighborhood. It's plain enough that, when young, you had an inquiring turn of mind—otherwise this characteristic would not have been so emphasized in the slight record we have of your adult life. For in practically every mention of you in Scripture, lo— you are asking a question!

Inquisitive concerning all things new, it is not surprising that you, with your partner Saint John, were among the first to set out for Bethania beyond the Jordan, to see for yourself what all this was about the strange, rugged prophet who, clad in the skins of wild animals, had begun to baptize in that territory. But when you found the Baptist he was already pointing to a Figure greater than he; and characteristically quick to take the hint, you at once set off with Saint John to follow that Figure. You can't deny that when you overtook Him, your first words were a question. "Master, where dwellest Thou?" you inquired. Your heart must have warmed at His ready welcome. "Come and see," He replied. And "they came, and saw where He abode—and they stayed with Him that day."

Enough to convince you was that one shining day, wasn't it, Saint Andrew? The next saw you breathlessly rushing off to Saint Peter with the glorious news that you had found the Messiah. It was charming, the way you saw to it that no time should be lost in enrolling your brother also under His banner—and how happily you both must have returned to your fishing with the assurance that He would soon come for you! At last dawned the great day when He, passing by the Sea of Galilee, called you from your nets to follow Him. Without hesitancy and with great joy, you accompanied Him from thence forward —but nevertheless, you continued to ask questions, Saint Andrew. And thus, perhaps, kept yourself better informed than any of the others. When that great multitude followed Him up upon the mountain and, having compassion on their hunger, He raised to the Twelve the problem of feeding them, it was only you, Saint Andrew, who must have been poking about in the crowd, and who could volunteer any accurate information concerning the state of the commissary.

"There is a boy here," you announced, "that hath five barley loaves and two fishes."

Now, if you had only let the matter rest there, I wouldn't accuse you of being a perpetual question mark. But you must perforce continue:

"But what are these among so many?"

Indeed, you were soon to learn just what they were, seeing them miraculously transformed into enough to feed five thousand, with twelve baskets of fragments left over—but did this wonderful lesson stop you from asking questions? Not at all, for one of the two remaining references to you in the Gospels, again definitely places you among the curious. You must remember the time when your Master predicted the total destruction of the Temple, and you, with three of the others, hastily took Him apart, importuning Him: "Tell us, when shall these things be? And what shall be the sign when all these things shall begin to be fulfilled?" The preponderance of evidence would lead us to believe that of that little group, it was your own inquisitive mind which suggested these queries.

There also seems to be reason for the supposition that the other Apostles, more reluctant to make inquiries, often put you up to finding out what they wished to know. I can almost hear them saying: "Now, Andrew, *you* ask Him!" Certain it is that at the time of that last tragic festival day in Jerusalem when the works of your Master were on everyone's tongue, and the city was full of pilgrims from all parts, "and there were certain Gentiles among them," who "therefore came to Philip . . . and desired him, saying: 'Sir, we would see Jesus,'" that "Philip cometh and telleth Andrew." He knew that you would have no hesitancy in asking the Master if He would receive them. Indeed, Saint Andrew, the more I think about you, the more I realize that you were perhaps the most useful in practical ways of all the Twelve. I see you as the head of the information-bureau—as one who, if he didn't know at the time, would soon find out! If making a journey I'm sure you had no silly pride about asking directions of strangers; I even imagine that you could inquire the age of a lady with such perfect *sangfroid* that she'd be startled into telling you.

But I think you must have grown a little weary as you became older (in truth, the sum of half your labors after your Lord's Resurrection would have sent to an early grave a dozen other men!) for, while I am loath to mention it, I seem to see a little tendency cropping up toward raising objections. Well, no wonder, after all you had been through in those first years, when you had toiled so valiantly in Judea to establish the Church—and later, after you had taken your chances with the rest in casting lots for the scene of your first foreign mission. The authorities differ as to exactly which land fell to you; but Origen, Eusebius, Saint Gregory of Nazianus, Chrysostom and Sophronius, Theodoret, and Nicephorus have all ventured an opinion on the matter; and between them they would have you the most widely traveled of all the Apostles. For you are credited with having evangelized Scythia, Epirus, Achaia, Hellas, Cappadocia, Galatia, Bithynia, Byzantium, Thrace, Macedonia, and Thessaly! To say nothing of the legends which claim that you labored in the "land of the Anthropophagi," the "land of the Kurds," and the "land beyond the Oasis"—which does indeed sound like the jumping-off place! My own modest opinion is that you visited all of them—at least, all that you could reach by boat.

As for this inclination of yours toward raising objections, while it's true that it is recounted only in the apocryphal accounts, nevertheless it is not entirely unconvincing. "The Acts of Andrew and Matthias" states that, when you were busy preaching in Achaia, your fellow-Apostle, Saint Matthew, laboring in far-away Myrmidonia (poor soul, he had unhappily drawn a cannibal-country in the lottery!) suddenly found himself in awkward difficulties. The first you knew of it was when your Lord appeared and announced that Matthew was imprisoned by the Myrmidonians. "For yet three days," you were alarmingly told, "and the men of the city will bring him forth and slay him for their food." You were bidden to set sail at once with your disciples, and go to his aid. You seemed to look somewhat dubiously upon this proposition. "My Lord," you demurred, "I shall not be able to accomplish the journey thither before the limited period of the three days; but send Thine angel quickly, that he may bring him out thence; for Thou knowest, Lord, that I also am flesh, and shall not be able to go there quickly." Why, Saint

Andrew! Didn't you know better by this time? But your objections availed naught, and you were commanded to "rise up early and go down to the sea," with your disciples. Rather reluctantly, I fear, you went—and there you found a nice little boat waiting, manned by three sailors. They told you they were bound for Myrmidonia —whereupon you admitted that you also had a mission there, but that, being disciples of Jesus Christ, you were rather cramped for funds, and could pay no passage money. The pilot replied that he preferred such passengers to those who could pay in gold, and forthwith invited you to step aboard. Then must have begun the most extraordinary voyage that you, experienced seaman though you were, had ever known. Refreshments were brought up from the hold, the pilot saying kindly: "Rise up, Brother, with thy friends; partake of food." One gathers that your poor disciples were not able to avail themselves of the invitation, having, it would seem, a touch of *mal-de-mer*—for the account states "they were not able to answer a word, for they were in distress because of the sea." But not you, the born sailor! I can see you eating heartily. When presently you came into lovely, placid waters, the pilot's method of steering fascinated you. Characteristically, you sought information:

85

"Tell me, O man, and show me the skill of thy steering; for I have never seen any man so steering in the sea, as I now see thee. For sixteen years have I sailed the sea, and behold, this is the seventeenth, and I have not seen such skill; for truly the boat is just as if on land. Show me, then, young man, thy skill."

But the pilot seemed to be much more interested in asking questions about your own work as an Apostle than in discussing his seamanship. After a delightful talk, your host "bent down his head upon one of the sailors and was quiet"— and you and your disciples were also soon fast asleep. How startled you must have been, Saint Andrew, to awaken and find yourself safely landed on the shores of Myrmidonia! The account states that then only did you realize that the boat had been handled by angels, and piloted by none other than your Master. But I feel sure that you must have had your suspicions all along. Apparently your objections had by this time completely vanished, for we are told that soon you were making the Sign of the Cross over Saint Matthew's prison, and that the guards fell unconscious as the doors swung open. You must have been somewhat surprised by the sight that greeted you, Saint Andrew. There was the interior full of quaking victims, each awaiting his

turn to be plumped into the cannibals' cauldron
—and there in the midst sat poor Saint Matthew,
actually singing (no doubt to keep up his courage!). "And having gone in, he found Matthew
sitting and singing—and seeing him, he stood up
and they saluted each other with a holy kiss."

I admire greatly the dispatch with which
you at once freed all the prisoners, sent Saint
Matthew safely off on a cloud, and yourself set
about converting the city. The former feats were
easy, compared to the latter; for apparently the
Myrmidonians were a tough lot. I shudder at
the way they dragged you about the streets for
three days until your "flesh stuck to the ground"
and your blood "flowed like water." But I rejoice
that eventually you were released, and were even
able to make a few converts. However, your hosts
had been, to say the least, fairly nerve-racking;
and no wonder you were anxious to see the last
of them! It was just too bad that when you tried
to make a quick get-away out of the city-gates,
your Lord suddenly appeared and directed you
to remain within seven extra days. Poor Saint
Andrew! Here again (and certainly not unrea-
sonably this time) you raised an objection. "I
must go to my disciples," you protested. But I'm
glad to see that you ended as usual, in doing as
you were told.

You had, certainly, a mind of your own and were never reluctant to speak it. Do you know that the story is still current of how, shortly after these events, when you were off with your brother Saint Peter on a little missionary jaunt, you suddenly found yourselves very hungry and with not a mite between you? It is related that you came upon an old man working in a field, of whom you begged something to eat. He must have been a very nice old man, Saint Andrew, for while he hadn't anything at hand to offer, he agreed to go into the city and buy some bread—provided you would keep an eye on his oxen and plough. This kindness pleased your brother so much that he suggested, as soon as the man's back was turned, that in his absence you both should till the field for him. You were so tired and hungry that you couldn't help raising this objection: "Father Peter," you said (though your brother, you had to address him thus because he was head of all the Apostles), "Father Peter, why dost thou bring toil upon us, especially when we have work enough already?" It did seem a bit unnecessary, didn't it, Saint Andrew? Yet in spite of this plaintive sigh, you nevertheless followed after Saint Peter with the seed as he took up the plough. When you had completed the task a remarkable thing happened. A great and golden harvest suddenly sprang up, and when the old man returned with food, he was overjoyed to see a rich field of waving grain where he had left but untilled earth. And behold—you had made another convert! With startling promptness had the "bread cast upon the waters" been returned.

But at least there was one time, Saint Andrew, when you raised no objection, nor asked any question—a time when you were so gloriously acquiescent that I'm sure your Master completely forgave you any previous obstructionism. That was when you met your martyrdom. We are told that you were imprisoned by the proconsul, Aegeas, in Patras of Achaia where you had made a host of converts; and that because you refused homage to the pagan gods you were condemned to die. It seems, also, that your thorough conversion of Maximilla, the proconsul's wife, as well as of Stratocles, his brother, had so enraged Aegeas that he took pleasure in planning the most lingering death he could devise. I often think of you, as you were led forth on that bleak November day, in the year A.D. 60, and beheld a cross at the place of execution. There were no objections now—you surprised all by breaking away from the guards and rushing joyously to embrace your cross. It mattered not to you that this cross was slightly different in shape than the one of Calvary, upon which He had died. It was yet a cross. Aegeas had ordered it shaped like an "X," so that you might be stretched as upon a rack—the better to be devoured by the wild dogs he meant to set upon you. But the wild dogs had more decency than he.

They left you unmolested—and there you hung for three days, happily smiling, and preaching to the people, who at length, recognizing your sanctity, grew bitter against the tyrant and demanded your release. It was quite like Aegeas, when the mob threatened him, to order his soldiers to take you down—but that was the last thing you wanted. You prayed to be allowed to complete your martyrdom; and the hands that reached up to unbind you fell helplessly at their owners' sides. Thus you died, murmuring: "Suffered under Pontius Pilate, and was crucified"— the phrase which tradition credits you with having contributed to the Apostles' Creed.

In view of all this, Saint Andrew, I hope you won't mind my mentioning that little tendency of yours toward raising objections. It occurs to me, rather late to be sure, that in doing so I only display that I possess the self-same trait. Why should I, forsooth, raise objections because you raised objections? However, I think

I shall do so anyway. For it's such a comforting thought to have—that I share something in common, if only a frailty, with Saint Andrew the Valorous!

NEVER MIND THEM,
SAINT THOMAS

NEVER MIND THEM,
SAINT THOMAS

I T ' s really been horrid of them, Saint Thomas, and for ever so long I've been wanting to tell you not to pay any attention. They haven't completely understood you, that's all—these people who would make you the greatest sceptic the world has ever known. When I think how much I have resented, during my life, their glib chatter about "doubting Thomases," I can appreciate how tiresome it must have been to you, through all the centuries. They've never let you forget for a second, that ill-advised statement: "Except I shall see in His hands, the print of the nails, and put my finger into the place of the nails, and put my hand into His side, I will not believe."

For the perpetuation of your much-exaggerated reputation as a sceptic, I suspect your fellow-Apostles themselves of being largely responsible. While I'm sure he didn't intend any mischief, it was Saint John, who, alone of the Evangelists, had to go and write all about that unfortunate episode; while the others, at least in the apocryphal accounts, were not above throwing it up to you from time to time. These probably gave the cue to succeeding generations, and indirectly prompted those mediæval mystery-plays to take many a mean dig at you for being a doubter. Certainly, within my own time and century, I have heard more hoary old agnostical sinners compared to you than I like to recall.

For my own part, I see you in quite a different light. It seems to me that this flat statement of yours which gave rise to all the unfavorable notoriety (and let's admit at once that, coming from one of the Twelve who had been privileged to witness countless proofs of His Divinity, it was something of a breath-taker) was not so much the fruit of scepticism as of another frailty —which, because I possess it myself, I would hasten to condone. Now come, Saint Thomas, let's both be perfectly frank and confess that we are nothing if not unpunctual. That weakness has certainly been largely at the root of all my own troubles, and I suspect it of having been responsible for many of yours.

In the first place, it seems almost certain that you had a date with the other Apostles, when, after the entombment of your Lord, "it was late that ... day, the first of the week, and the doors were shut where the Apostles were gathered together." Just what detained you, or where you were, is annoyingly omitted, but anyway I have a feeling that, knowing the circumstances, I, at least, would understand. Probably there was no hour-glass handy, or you may have gotten tangled up in traffic. In any case, you failed to keep your appointment. Yet your Master gave you every opportunity (not that you or any of your companions knew He was coming) for it is expressly stated, "when it was *late* that day . . . Jesus came and stood in the midst, and said to them: 'Peace be to you.' "

It was a wonderful experience for your heart-sore and frightened companions gathered in that upper room, and of course they were bound, with no little exuberance, to tell you all about it. From your reaction, I even suspect them of a touch of that human, "now-see-what-you-missed" attitude. For certainly something threw you into an antagonistic mood. I have so often felt likewise, Saint Thomas, when secretly annoyed at being so tardy as to miss the best part of the programme—an impulse to say to those irritatingly punctual persons, that I did not believe I had missed so much after all! Poor Saint Thomas—you were properly and publicly humiliated for this attitude, when, eight days later, you did keep your appointment in the upper room, and your Lord again came. "Put in thy, finger hither, and see My hands," He said to you, "and bring hither thy hand, and put it into My side; and be not faithless but believing." You replied, simply: "My Lord and my God!"—an ultimate, beautiful, and perfect act of faith.

It must have been that, then and there, He forgave you your previous churlishness—even though thereafter succeeding Christian generations would never let you forget it! And this in spite of the tradition that your own special contribution to the Apostles' Creed was that superb revocation of your early, lamentable speech: "And the third day, He arose again from the dead."—Some people are never satisfied, Saint Thomas.

Perhaps there are those who will argue that this episode of the upper room is not enough to justify my contention that you were really an unpunctual soul. But there is also another story, which, even though it appears only in the apocryphal "Passing of the Blessed Virgin Mary," is still no less convincing to one who, admiring you greatly, is determined to unearth at least one trait in common with you. Therein it is related that, when the appointed time came for the Mother of your Lord to die, all the Apostles were scattered far and wide. It being revealed to them that her earthly hour had come, all but you somehow got themselves immediately transported over vast areas to the door of her chamber. Of course you, away off in India, also wished to be there—perhaps even more than the others, for it is said that a particular friendship existed between you and Mary; but it seems that you were about to say Mass when the tidings came. You probably thought you would have time, first to say the Mass, and then be off; at any rate, you began the service. To your surprise, in the midst of it, a cloud came along and unceremoniously bore you off—sacerdotal robes and all! Meanwhile, the Blessed Mother had died and been reverently buried by the other Apostles. But she, as always, understood you. Knowing you would be chagrined at arriving too late, she appeared to you as she was carried up into Heaven. Graciously she smiled down upon you, and tossed you her scarf as a loving memento. Glowing from this experience, you finally reached the others, only to be upbraided by Saint Peter —whom one can't really blame for being a bit upset at this repetition of your customary tardiness.

When your friends explained that they had already buried Mary, to their consternation you announced that she was not where they had laid her. This was even more irritating than your tardiness. "Were you forever to be a doubter?" they demanded. But you stuck to your point. "Then, as it were in a rage, they went to the sepulchre," just to prove you were wrong. Save for a profusion of crimson roses and white lilies, they found it empty—equally to their mortification and your own satisfaction. And "all asked pardon of the Blessed Thomas." Thus, after all those years, you eventually had the edge on them. You may have missed out that first time, but now you could claim to be the sole witness of a great vision, and for proof you could display that precious token given you by Our Lady herself.

Unpunctual you were—and you had the intrepidity of the best of the unpunctual. For who shall deny that it requires no small amount of bravery to be forever late? Not another Apostle is credited in the Gospels with as magnificent an act of courage as you displayed on that occasion when your Master and His companions, driven by the fierce hostility raging in and about Jerusalem, had withdrawn into the country beyond the Jordan. There news reached your Lord that Lazarus, who lived with his sisters, Martha and Mary, close to the inflamed city, was ill. "Now Jesus loved Martha, and her sister Mary, and Lazarus." Two days later, He announced to you all plainly that Lazarus had died. "Let us," He said, "go into Judea again." This proposition seems to have struck no end of terror into the hearts of your companions. "Rabbi," they pled, "the Jews but now sought to stone Thee; and goest Thou thither again?" Patiently, the Master told them: "Lazarus our friend, sleepeth; but I go that I may awake him out of sleep." A frightened silence followed. Probable death, they knew, awaited them all, should they follow Him back to Judea. It was almost as though they had determined, if bent upon this journey, He must go alone—when you spoke.

"Let us also go," you cried to your fellow-Apostles, "that we may die with Him!" It was like a magnificent trumpet-call sounded to a routed and retreating army. You, alone, had turned the tide. Death you undoubtedly expected to meet, for this act of loyalty—but death was worth it, as far as you were concerned. Shamefacedly, the others agreed; and soon the little company had their faces staunchly set toward Jerusalem the vindictive. And Lazarus, who had been dead four days, was brought gloriously back to life in the sight of an astounded multitude.

In view of all this, it seems so stupid of people to be continually calling you "Doubting

Thomas." They should really think of you as "Courageous (if a bit tardy) Thomas."

And now I am reminded of something that has long puzzled me, Saint Thomas, and I do wish you'd enlighten me. Repeatedly you are referred to in the Gospels as "Thomas, who is called Didymus." For years I thought this nothing but a rather derogatory nickname, and I resented it fiercely for your sake. I wouldn't have minded so much, if it had been pretty. But Didymus! It has such a flippant, undignified sound. And then, suddenly one day, I stumbled upon the knowledge that Didymus, in Aramaic, signifies "twin"! Thomas, the Twin, it appears you were —and now I can't sleep nights for wondering what ever happened to the other twin. And whether it was brother or sister; and whether (for twins are so devoted) you had heartbrokenly left him or her, to follow your Master? If you did, I'm sure you at length received an even more wonderful reward than the others. For didn't He promise: "And every one that hath left ... brethren ... for My Name's sake, shall receive an hundredfold, and shall possess life everlasting"? So much for leaving brethren—but for those who left a twin for His sake, there would naturally be an even greater reward!

Although no mention is made of it, I have a

feeling that you and Saint Andrew were particularly congenial—you were so much alike. Both of you were valorous, and both of you had a way of asking questions and raising objections. I'm sure that, no matter how the others felt, Andrew, at least, understood you when, at the Last Supper, your Lord having just said: "Whither I go, you know, and the way you know," you looked puzzled and protested: "Lord, we know not whither Thou goest; and how can we know the way?" You were nothing if not literal, Saint Thomas—poor dear, there was so much that was difficult to understand, wasn't there? And not only literal were you, but also very practical—for it is alleged that you were a carpenter, having mastered the trade in your native Galilee, a craft that had trained you to trust only accurate figures and measures by rule. For this cause is your symbol in early Church art the measuring-stick. Of course it must have bothered you at first that you could not mathematically apply it to the wonderful things you were being taught. But when at length He arose from the dead, and thus gave your practical mind a permanent jolt, you were as eager as the others to spread His mystical message, what though somewhat "choosy" as to the exact place you would spread it!

As you probably know, "The Acts of the

Holy Apostle Thomas," one of the oldest pieces of Syriac literature, states that you preached, eventually, to a varied assortment of peoples—the Parthians, the Medes, the Persians, the Germans, the Hyrcanians, the Bactrians, and the Bardians (whoever they may have been). It is even suggested that you came to America. Lew Wallace wrote a charming book, "The Fair God," around that lovely tradition. It would have been quite in line with your valor to have done so. As for me, I'm so disappointed that the weight of authority seems to discredit this view. In any case, we are told in the apocryphal accounts that you objected strenuously to the locale of your first assignment.

It was India.—One delightful legend relates that your Master, before His death, journeyed there to pay a visit to the Wise Men who, many years before, had brought gifts to His cradle in Bethlehem. Of the original three, only two survived at that time—Melchior and Baltazar. These aged rulers welcomed Him joyfully, and on His departure, begged Him to send them one of His own disciples to preach to all their people. The Master promised He would, and settled upon you for choice. "The Acts of Thomas," however, would give a different reason for your orders to India. It is claimed therein that, after your

Lord's Resurrection, one King Gundaphoros of that country, a rich and mighty potentate, desired to build a fairer palace for himself than had ever been seen in the land. Like many kings, he decided that only an imported architect would do. So he dispatched his merchant, Abbanes, on a far journey to find such a craftsman—and Abbanes at length sauntered into the marketplace where you were. Simultaneously, your Master appeared, and told you that you must go to India. To which you protested: "And how can I, being an Hebrew man, go among the Indians to proclaim the truth?" When reassured on this point (it's really very distasteful to me, to continue the account, Saint Thomas, but I suppose we may as well make a clean breast of it) you began to put up excuses anent the "weakness of the flesh" (were you, perhaps, subject to malaria?) and you finally came out flatfootedly with the statement:

"Wherever Thou wishest to send me, send me elsewhere; for to the Indians I am not going!"

Saint Thomas! Your Master would see about that. At this point Abbanes approached, inquiring for a carpenter, and your Lord indicated you as His slave, and a master at the building trade. When pinned right down to it, you had to admit that you were, indeed, His slave—and to submit in silence as He sold you, for three pounds of uncoined silver, to the Indian merchant. Off you had to sail with Abbanes; and after many days and many adventures, you reached the kingdom of Gundaphoros, who at once asked you what you knew how to build. You replied (somewhat airily, I'm afraid): "In wood, ploughs, yokes, balances, pulleys, and boats and oars and masts; and in hewn stone, monuments, temples, and palaces for kings!" Gundaphoros was delighted, and commanded you to draw up plans for a castle, which you did in masterly fashion. You "set the doors toward the rising of the sun, to look to the light; and the windows toward its setting, to the winds; and made the bake-house to be toward the south, and the water-tank, for abundance, toward the north." Overjoyed at your wisdom, the King directed:

"Begin to build!"

But of course you had an objection. "I cannot," you declared, "build at this time."

"When," demanded disappointed royalty, "when wilt thou be able?"

"I shall begin," you stated, with all the finality of a union-carpenter, "in Dius [October] and end in Xanthicus" [April].

"But," feebly protested Gundaphoros, "that is not the usual time for building!"

"That may well be," you firmly replied, "but it is *my* time!"

And that was that. The King chewed his royal finger-nails and waited—even as kings must ever wait, on labor. Unfortunately for him, about the time you were ready to start the work, he was called away on a far journey, but he left in your hands a large amount of gold to defray all construction costs, stretching his budget to do so.

"This," you said to yourself, "would be much better expended on the poor, than on any royal palace." And forthwith you began to divert all funds toward feeding the hungry and clothing the naked. Not a sou did you keep for yourself— but neither did you add one stone to the royal edifice! And the poor had a perfectly grand time. When Gundaphoros at length returned, and found all his money spent and no sign of a palace, he naturally made a scene. His people hastened to tell him: "Thomas continually fasts and prays, and eats only bread with salt, and his drink is water; and he carries one coat, whether in warm weather or in cold; and he takes nothing from anyone, but gives to others even what he has." But this in no way appeased the furious monarch. He had you thrown into prison and you were about to be flayed alive, when a surprising thing happened. The King's brother, Prince Gad, suddenly fell ill and died.

As it all came out later, when Gad's soul arrived in Paradise, the first thing he beheld was the most magnificent palace imaginable. So lavish was it, that he, a prince, craved only to be allowed to lie in one of its "lower chambers". But the angels forbade him, saying the palace was the property of his brother, King Gundaphoros, built up in Heaven for him by you, Saint Thomas, as you dispensed his wealth in almsdeeds on earth. Now Prince Gad, it would appear, was a sharp business man, even in death, for he said to the angels: "I entreat you, my Lords, permit me to go to my brother, that I may buy this palace from him—for my brother does not know what it is like, and he will sell it to me!" I cannot believe, Saint Thomas, that the angels, in allowing him to return to earth, were being parties to this shrewd scheme. Rather, it seems certain that they saw an outcome not then visible to Gad. The latter, suddenly coming to life in his burial robe, hastened to tell his royal brother all about the palace in Paradise. It would seem that, shrewd as Gad was, Gundaphoros was shrewder—for he plied the Prince with the most searching questions, and as a result grew so convinced of your sanctity, that he released you from prison and himself became a Christian! When Gad saw he had lost the real-estate deal, he followed the King's example, and together they gave all their worldly goods to the poor.

Alas, that after this first marvelous success with royalty, you should finally meet your death at the hands of an Indian monarch! But you will say, "Alas, nothing!", since that death was a martyr's, and the sort you preferred to all others—to be able to lay down your life for the love of your Lord. It is related that you eventually got into hot water with King Mesdeus, who did not approve of your wholesale conversion of his entire household. Regarding you as a sorcerer, he had his soldiers take you up on a distant mountain, where the people, whose hearts you had won, would not be able to witness his cruelty—and there you were speared to death.— "And all the brethren wept, and wrapped him up in beautiful shawls . . . and laid him in the tomb in which of old, the kings used to be buried."

Many are the charming stories which connect your labors with India, Saint Thomas, and even those who doubt them admit that there still exists in the southern part of that land a large group of people who proudly call themselves "Thomas Christians". They claim that they are faithfully preserving the Faith as you taught it to their forefathers almost two thousand years ago. In view of all you accomplished, not only in this way, but also in the wonderful miracles you wrought, it's really ridiculous of people to speak of you as though you had never done anything but doubt! Never mind them, Saint Thomas.

Just how long you were permitted to rest in that first tomb, wrapped up in those lovely Indian shawls, is a question only you can settle—for tradition has disagreed woefully on this point, although it is accepted as fact that eventually some of your bones were transported to Edessa in Mesopotamia. Over their possession warred the Infidels and the Crusaders, and finally the Crusaders carried them off to the Island of Chios. Poor Saint Thomas! For yet again were they disturbed when Manfred, Prince of Taranto, had his fleet carry them off to Ortona, in Italy, where they were placed in a great cathedral. Even after all this, the Turks sacked Ortona and rifled your tomb for suspected treasure. But the pious Italians restored all they could—and thus ended, let us hope, the long continued disturbance to your peace.

But, at least, all accounts agree that at your tomb, wherever it happened to be for the moment, were wonderful miracles wrought. And while you remained in it in India, you received the dressiest callers, Saint Thomas! They hailed from all over the world. Came Theodore, the Gaul, in the sixth century; came Bishops Swithelm and Aethelstane, emissaries of Alfred the Great, three hundred years later; came Marco Polo some four hundred years after, reporting that: "The body of Messer Saint Thomas, the Apostle, lies in this province of Malabar, at a certain little town having no great population. ... Both Christians and Saracens, however, greatly frequent it in pilgrimage."

The only dressy caller who may have at all dismayed you, was a certain lady-author. She visited you in the fourth century, being the writer of "Peregrinatio ad Loca Sancta". That was bad enough—but she had to disturb your much-needed rest by reading aloud for hours over your tomb! It is said that she was either Sylvia of Aquitaine, or Etheria of Spain (either name would brand her as a lady-author) and I very much fear she was an abbess. The reason I am severe with her is that she got there first—I mean, before I did—and since her reading consisted of the same material concerning your life which I am at present reviewing for you, I am afraid from sheer ennui, you will say: "Preserve me from any more lady-authors!"

Now, if it hadn't been for Sylvia or Etheria

—well, you might feel gentler toward me. And when I think of the undoubtedly powerful influence you wield in the celestial courts, all I can say, Saint Thomas, is that I'm relying upon your reputation as a gentleman and as a saint!

THE LADIES LIKED YOU, SAINT PHILIP!

THE LADIES LIKED YOU,
SAINT PHILIP!

Now please don't take offense, Saint Philip —you of Bethsaida of Galilee, and one of the most delightful of the delightful Twelve— when I say the ladies liked you. For I intend it as a compliment—being a lady myself. Perhaps you won't think I am, when you've finished reading this missive—but if I listen to such fears, I'll never get anywhere with it.

I could never understand why those of your own sex have always considered it a reflection on a man, to have it said of him that he was liked by the ladies. That attitude is just one more masculine and deplorable dig at the expense of women, implying as it does that any object of the ladies' esteem must necessarily be of utterly no account—that the ladies, in other words, haven't enough sense to come in out of the rain. Whereas you and I agree that they are really creatures of superior mentality—to me, at least, conclusively proved by the fact that they liked you so much. And you liked them, also, and still achieved sainthood—which many will say was a remarkable accomplishment. But we both know that the one is just a logical step toward the other.

The reason I'm sure the ladies liked you is because there seem to have been more of them in your life than in that of any other Apostle. They simply wouldn't have been there if they hadn't been fond of you! You may, perhaps, have somewhat deplored their presence until that time when you put them in their proper place, and got them assiduously working for your Master—in which, indeed, you were wonderfully successful. Now, as far as I can count, there were at least five women intimately associated with your earthly existence—and I presume most men would assure me that that was plenty! There was your wife—there were your three daughters—and there was your sister, Mariamme. To be sure, little is said about your wife, but as you know, the tradition in patristic literature is markedly to the effect that you were a married man—and Bishop Polycrates of Ephesus once wrote a letter to Saint Victor in which he said that you had three daughters. As for your sister, Mariamme, it is well known that she was most devoted to you, and that, after the Resurrection, she accompanied you on all your missionary journeys. Indeed, as a tribute to her holy coöperation in your

own great work, the Greek Church canonized her
—which I'm sure must have pleased you very
much, Saint Philip. It would seem that your
daughters, too, remained close to you during your
life, and that you were always their guide and
spiritual inspiration. For Polycrates declared in
that letter, that "Philip . . . is buried in Hierapolis, with his two daughters, who grew old as
virgins"; and that a third daughter "led a life
in the Holy Ghost, and rests in Ephesus."

Had your sister and daughters vanished
from the scene after your Lord called you to re-
nounce the material pleasures of this world, I
should not be so sure the ladies liked you. But
they seem to have stuck as close as you would
allow them, Saint Philip—and hence I'm certain
you were one who had a particular understanding
of women. It is presumed that your wife died
before you began your active life as an Apostle
—and, of course, some scholars have fussily declared that there is some doubt about your having had three daughters. They point to that other
Philip, the deacon and evangelist, who went you
one better it seems, and had four daughters—
prophetesses, at that—who were also buried in
Hierapolis. It is claimed that the early writers
confused you two, but I'm convinced that Bishop
Polycrates was a careful man, and sure of his

facts—and he specifically states: "Philip, one of the Twelve Apostles...with his...daughters." Now, it's just because of all this petticoat influence that I'm daring to write you, Saint Philip. It makes me feel, no matter what I say, that you will understand. You see, the ladies liked you—and they still like you. Let us hope you don't object.

Personally, I have a perfectly lovely time, thinking about you. I can picture, for instance, your life as a child in your native Bethsaida, that cheerful little town on the shores of Lake Genesareth, busy with its fishermen and boats. It must have been a wonderful place, for it produced you and Saint Peter and Saint Andrew—three of that extraordinary Twelve. I wonder if I am mistaken, in imagining that you three were frequent companions on fishing trips and pleasure excursions—in fact, that you with your friend Bartholomew may have actually set out with them and Saint John upon that journey to hear the Baptist, who was preaching "beyond Jordan". Certain it is that you, Saint Philip, were not far away when that great, gaunt figure pointed out the Messiah to Andrew and John—and when Andrew brought Peter to the Master. "On the following day, He would go forth into Galilee," wrote Saint John, "and He findeth Philip." So it is clear that your

Lord first looked upon you in Bethania. "And Jesus saith to him, 'Follow Me.'"

It is charming to think how simply and how happily you did so, Saint Philip—and to reflect upon your enthusiasm and generosity in immediately wanting to share the great privilege that had come to you, with your friend, Bartholomew —or Nathanael, as he was also called. All through the Gospel story, and all through tradition, runs the hint of your friendship for him. There is so much I would like to ask you, for instance, about how you first came to know each other, and what were the ties that bound you before that last and strongest one was formed—the one that held you both fast, forever after, to Him. Saint John tells us that, as soon as your Lord called you, you sought out Bartholomew, and said: " 'We have found Him of Whom Moses in the law, and the prophets did write—Jesus, the son of Joseph of Nazareth!' " And so you brought your friend to the Master. You must have been very happy when Bartholomew at once threw in his lot with you as one of His followers.

Is it not true, Saint Philip, that thereafter you two were much together? For Saint Matthew, Saint Mark, and Saint Luke all couple your names in the lists of the Twelve, and imply that, when He sent them out, "two and two", to preach

in His Name, you and Bartholomew journeyed
together. It is delightful to read in the apocryphal accounts that this sympathetic companion-
ship endured all your life. Even at your death, so
they relate, this friend was near; himself suffering and tortured by the hands that were martyr-
ing you. So it is that I think of you, Saint Philip,
not only as the Apostle whose life was most
concerned with women—but also as the one of
whom is recorded the warmest friendship for another man. Cynics will claim that this was only
reasonable—that having five women to contend
with at home, you needed a male friend far worse
than did any of the others! But I feel sure that
your friendship for Bartholomew was only another proof of your capacity for sympathy.

To me, you've always seemed a very warm-
hearted person, naturally drawing others to you
by your own attractive personality. Your in-
stincts must have been social; and I can imagine,
when the Master and you, and Peter, Andrew,
John and Bartholomew were all invited to that
wedding in Cana, that you, at least, "accepted
with pleasure". You liked weddings—for hadn't
you participated in one yourself? And I think
you must have been the merriest of the guests
gathered around that festive board which presently was to witness His "beginning of miracles",

and to see the pale, listless water transformed into rich, ruby wine.

Although after that first manifestation of His power, you were almost exclusively occupied with spiritual values, yet I see the amiable sociability which naturally marked you, never quite submerged. I am thinking of that time much later, when were gathered in Jerusalem to observe the festival day, your Master and the Twelve, and pilgrims from all Judea. "There were," Saint John wrote, "certain Gentiles among them." In the crowded Hebrew capital, thronging with believing Jews, these must indeed have felt as strangers in a strange city. Yet they had but to listen to the common talk in the marketplace, to learn the news on everyone's tongue—of the Prophet Who wrought such miracles, and Who was, even then, present in that very city. They burned with curiosity to see this One, of Whom such wonders were recounted—but with their request to meet Him, it was only you, Saint Philip, out of all the Twelve, whom they dared approach. It would seem as though they had heard, of that little company which surrounded Him, that you were the friendliest toward strangers. "These therefore came to Philip... and desired him, saying: 'Sir, we would see Jesus.'" I'm sure, kindly as you were, that you wanted ever so much to gain them the privilege; but nevertheless you did not wish to impose unnecessarily upon your Master's strength, so taxed every day by the clamoring crowds. It is pleasant to think how in your dilemma you turned for counsel to your old friend Andrew. "Philip cometh, and telleth Andrew." Andrew was accustomed to having things put up to him, and apparently he, too, sympathized with these strangers—for "again, Andrew and Philip told Jesus."

It seems to me, because you were, more than the others, a "family man", that you have deserved a sympathy that has not usually been accorded you. It must have taken a keen practical sense to provide for those five women, and at the same time be engaged in a project remote from material gain. But, somehow, you managed both successfully. And I, a woman, envy you your domestic ability—for who but a good housekeeper could have so quickly and so accurately gauged the amount of money it would take to feed all those people who had followed Him across the Sea of Tiberias? "When Jesus therefore had lifted up His eyes, and seen that a very great multitude cometh to Him, He said to Philip: 'Whence shall we buy bread that these may eat?'" Rapidly you surveyed the crowd, and as rapidly indulged in practical mental arithmetic. "Philip answered Him: 'Two hundred penny-worth of bread is not sufficient for them, that every one may take a little.'" You knew, didn't you, Saint Philip? Not for nothing had you fed those five women all these years! But it was as though your Master, knowing that this must occasionally have been a strain on your resources, and had worried you, was determined to give you a lesson in the futility of measuring things by the penny-worth, when there was, even for such mundane matters as fish and bread, a far more efficacious mode at hand. For Saint John says that in asking His question of you, He did so merely to "try" you—"for He Himself knew what He would do." With five barley loaves and two fishes, He amply fed five thousand. What, indeed, was a mere detail like feeding five women? His action said in so many words: "Cease worrying over your silly domestic responsibilities, Philip!"

But it would seem as though your practical side could not even thus be downed. For at that last, sadly beautiful meal, just before He died, when you sat about the board with the Master and the others, it again popped out. You will remember that your Lord declared to the company: "If you had known Me, you would without doubt have known My Father also: and from henceforth you shall know Him, and you have seen Him." Even after all that had passed, this did not make much sense to your practical mind, for you blurted out: "Lord, shew us the Father, and it is enough for us!" Now, whatever made you say such a thing, even if you were thinking it, Saint Philip? I'm sure you regretted the words as soon as they were out of your mouth, and that you felt you deserved far worse than His gentle rebuke: "Have I been so long a time with you; and have you not known Me? Philip, he that seeth Me, seeth the Father also. How sayest thou, 'Shew us the Father'? Do you not believe that I am in the Father, and the Father in Me? Otherwise believe for the very works' sake." You had forgotten, for the moment, that wonderful wedding party in Cana—all the lame who had since been made to walk—all the deaf who had been made to hear—all the blind who had been made to see—and, finally, the very dead who had been made to live!

But because you were Philip, I say (and I'm sure all the ladies will say) that this was an understandable lapse. (Though I hope you won't mention the matter of my special sympathy for you to dear Saint Peter. He might not understand. I've been so utterly devoted to him for so many years—and I wouldn't want him to think me fickle.) If any should comment unfavorably upon this remark of yours at the Last Supper, I'm sure they would be men—but even in such an event I know you'd be tolerant, for you and I both understand how men just sometimes cannot seem to help a little fault-finding at the expense of one whom the ladies greatly admire. We suspect the real reason, don't we, Saint Philip?

Not even the gentlemen, though, could find a single thing to criticize in your behavior after your Lord had risen. You led a zealous and a holy life, laboring manfully and courageously to spread the Gospel. Before your chance was cast in that lottery which was to determine the place of labor for each of the Twelve, you abode with the rest in that upper room in Jerusalem, and took your turn at debate with the Jews on the Temple steps. "The Recognitions of Clement" relates how one of the Scribes sought to refute your doctrine by claiming that your Lord had not wrought His miracles as a prophet, but as a magician. I should have loved being there, Saint Philip, to hear you, as the account states, "eagerly encounter" him. He hadn't, apparently, a leg left to stand on, when you got through with him.

I wonder how you felt when that Apostolic lottery accorded you the land of Scythia—which Papias and Nicephorus both agree was the locale of your first missionary labor? Being the sociable person you were, I imagine that any place where there were people would have suited you. I like to think of you as you set forth—your sister, Mariamme, trotting faithfully at your side—and perhaps your three daughters bringing up the rear. For if two of them were buried with you at the end, these at least must certainly have been with you during part of your missionary career. You may have tried (though never successfully, if we are to take the word of Polycrates) to marry them off. After all, what could husbands offer them that would compare with the beautiful life they led with their Aunt Mariamme, and their wonderful father? These children must have been very happy to witness your success in founding all those Eastern churches—and, if Eusebius is right, in Christianizing the Hellenic world. You kept them traveling, for "The Acts of Philip" states that, about the time Trajan became Emperor of Rome, "Philip, the Apostle, going through the cities and regions of Lydia and Asia, preached to all, the Gospel of Christ."

It was only, according to the apocryphal accounts, when you got to Hierapolis of Phrygia, that real trouble began. You remember how you found that city totally given over to idolatry of the most loathsome form—the worship of the serpent.

Now I wonder if its regeneration seemed so difficult that you were forced to send for your good friend, Bartholomew? For tradition has it that he joined you there. You all might have had a very pleasant visit with Stachys, who gladly opened his house to you, if that old serpent, coiled up under the altar of the temple, hadn't been so popular. To be sure, you drew crowds to the house of Stachys, and were greatly assisted by Mariamme, of whom the account states: "And Philip's sister, Mariamme, sitting in the entry of the house of Stachys, addressed herself to those coming, and persuaded them to listen to the Apostles." I'm sure you and Bartholomew appreciated her efforts at drumming up trade, and were grateful for all the converts she drew in—until it came to the Lady Nicanora. Not that Nicanora, herself, wasn't a very charming person. But I think you'll agree with me, Saint Philip, that her husband was otherwise—and wasn't it unfortunate that he also happened to be the all-powerful Roman proconsul! What an old nuisance he was! Have you perchance ever seen the story as the apocryphal record gives it?

It relates that Nicanora, already predisposed to Christianity, was lying ill in bed, when she heard you were in town. "And rising up, she went forth out of her house through the side door" (one presumes she didn't dare use the front door!) "carried by her own slaves in a silver litter, and went into the house of Stachys. . . . And behold, there came the tyrant, the husband of Nicanora, rageing like an unbroken horse" (he must have been a pretty sight, Saint Philip!) "and having laid hold of his wife's garments, he cried out, saying: 'O Nicanora, did I not leave thee in bed?' " The mean old thing had probably rejoiced in the illness which had kept her there a prisoner! Wasn't he horrid, Saint Philip, to be so incensed because you cured her? But Nicanora wasn't afraid—and you must have been delighted when she answered him back, saying she had become a Christian. "And when the gloomy tyrant . . . heard these words . . . he seized her by the hair of her head, and dragged her along, kicking her." What a charming gentleman! And apparently poor Nicanora never even cried, "ouch!" Of course you knew, right then and there, Saint Philip, that the dickens would be to pay. But you, Mariamme, and Bartholomew were all ready to meet it. Poor things, how I hate to think of the way the proconsul tortured you, and how he had you dragged through the streets to be imprisoned in that awful temple of the serpent! There seems to me a certain symbolism in the fact that you, alone of the Apostles, bitterly experienced the enmity of a serpent —and that all womankind has suffered from such. It's another bond of sympathy between you and the ladies, Saint Philip.

There is a legend which declares that you held a cross before the idolatrous altar sheltering that huge snake, and· commanded it to come forth. Obediently, it did—but you couldn't have been exactly happy over your success, for the story goes that the serpent was anything but perfumed. In fact, it is said that many witnesses fell dead from that dreadful odor. You were kept quite busy, it would appear, restoring them to life—but even these good offices could not move the heart of that "gloomy tyrant", the proconsul. I imagine you felt worse over the sentence he passed upon your sister and your friend, than over the one he imposed upon you—though you knew the latter meant certain death. Poor, holy Mariamme, it is related, was publicly to be stripped naked—but your prayers miraculously enveloped her with a cloud of fire in which she remained invisible and unharmed. It must have been horrible for you to see Bartholomew nailed to the temple gate—and what fiendish cruelty, to arrange your own place of torture right opposite his, so that you two devoted friends would have to gaze upon each other's suffering! There stretched unhappy Bartholomew, quailing the while at the sight of you, as you hung, head down, pierced by iron hooks, and suspended by the ankles!

It was like you to plead with the people to release Bartholomew (which they eventually did) but to insist on consummating your own martyrdom. I shall always think of you there, preaching your Lord's Gospel with the last breath that remained in your body—and at length converting the entire, idolatrous populace. There is, somehow, so much pathos in your last remarks to your beloved Bartholomew. "And lay your peace upon the house of Stachys, as Christ laid His peace upon this city." Even in that black hour, you were not forgetful of the hospitality this friend had given you and yours. The heartbroken Bartholomew must have wept, as you begged him not to have your body bound in cloth—"because," you said, "the body of my Lord was wrapped in linen." It was not fitting, you felt, that yours should be cared for in the same manner. "Syriac sheets of paper," and "papyrus reeds," were good enough for you.

It was a glorious death, Saint Philip. And there, weeping at the end, stood the two who, at least to me, symbolize your entire life—your friend, Bartholomew, and your sister, Mariamme. You had understood how to be a faithful friend to men—and you had known how to be gentle and understanding with women. Indeed, whenever I think upon all the things reviewed in this letter, Saint Philip, I say to myself: "Well, no wonder the ladies liked him!"

WITHOUT GUILE,
BUT NOT WITHOUT STYLE,
SAINT BARTHOLOMEW!

WITHOUT GUILE,
BUT NOT WITHOUT STYLE,
SAINT BARTHOLOMEW!

IT'S a very pleasant shock, Saint Bartholomew —fifth chosen of that exclusive and utterly charming company of Twelve—to discover that you had a fondness for clothes! Such a predilection seems inextricably woven in my own warp and woof (I hope this letter isn't going to make you feel that I have too much warp) and hence it's comforting to learn that it may not, in all cases, be entirely incompatible with sanctity. Now of course I know that most hagiological opinion is markedly to the contrary—but that's because it has never properly considered your own splendid sartorial solicitude, Saint Bartholomew.

After all, I'm sure the pagans, whom you set out to win over to your Master's cause, found it very pleasant to look upon a well-dressed Apostle. Not that I've discovered any complaints about the clothing the others wore—only human nature, being what it is, always welcomes most readily those who are pleasing to its physical eye.

And you certainly were that, Saint Bartholomew!

Although some churlish souls may perhaps complain that there is no Scriptural assurance to this effect, yet if they should deny that tradition can very often be founded on fact, don't you agree that they would be taking half the joy out of life? Now, if it were just a wisp of tradition, my theory about you might be shamed into silence; but when the matter has been gone into with such detail by the Ante-Nicene Fathers, it seems reasonable to conclude that it must have had some basis in truth. So I'm putting it up to you, Saint Bartholomew, to reassure me that the account in "The Martyrdom of the Holy and Glorious Apostle Bartholomew" is correct. For it would disappoint me terribly to have to relinquish that charming picture of you!

But perhaps you have never seen that passage which recounts how certain idolaters, some years after you had set forth to carry your Lord's Gospel to the uttermost parts of the earth, were disturbed by the fact that their god, Astaruth, had suddenly ceased to bestow favors. So they journeyed to another city, where was enshrined an even more powerful deity, one Becher—and appealed to him to explain Astaruth's strange inefficiency. Becher answered them plainly:

"Since God has sent His Apostle, Bartholomew, into that temple, your Astaruth is held fast by chains of fire, and can no longer either speak or breathe." To their knowledge, the questioners had never seen you—for you were living incognito, among the pilgrims and the poor sheltered by that temple. So they at once inquired of Becher what you looked like. That deity replied impressively:

"He is clothed with a white undercloak, which is bordered with purple—and upon his shoulders hangs a very white cloak!"

Now, that was certainly a most beautiful "ensemble," Saint Bartholomew. White and purple, combined properly, are always exceedingly smart. No one can make me believe that this costume had not been carefully planned—nor that you were one who gave no thought to clothes.

Further, I do wish you'd tell me if Becher's next remarks have been accurately reported. "Bartholomew's clothes," he confided, "have been worn twenty-six years—but neither are they dirty, nor have they waxed old!" Saint Bartholomew, *if* so—won't you please tell me, *how* so? If only I could learn your method, it would save such endless trouble. I should love to be able to keep a white garment in use for twenty-six years, and yet utterly spotless. Now probably, you had very sensibly ordered that purple border put around the bottom, where things get soiled most rapidly—yet even this practical forethought could not have kept the white part clean for so many years. But, I expect you'll tell me that one has to be at least an Apostle to accomplish such a feat. So I suppose there's no use asking how it can be done.

Yes, indeed, your clothes had style—and from the further words of Becher I can see how well you wore them. He stated that you had "black hair, a shaggy head, a fair skin, large eyes, beautiful nostrils, his ears hidden by the hair of his head" (that made it nice in cold weather, Saint Bartholomew) "with a yellow beard and a few grey hairs." Perhaps it may annoy you to have your personal appearance thus discussed so frankly—but anyone as good-looking as you, should be accustomed to such words and able to ignore them without embarrassment. Personally, I cannot help reflecting what a charming appearance you must have made—certainly, an "eyeful" to those pagans in far-away India whom you had set out to convert. Half the battle was won before you even opened your mouth. Super-salesmen of today, who get themselves up in sartorial perfection before visiting customers, are only, after all, stealing your own wise thunder, Saint Bartholomew.

If this is how you appeared some years after your Lord's Resurrection, you must indeed have been a very handsome youth when you first pledged your life to Him. I only wish I knew more about you; but it would seem, in spite of your good looks and dressy appearance, that you were really a very modest person. In the Gospel story, you cling, I suspect purposely, to a misty background—as though you considered yourself the least among His followers. We only know that you were born in Cana of Galilee, of Jewish parents—and really called at first Nathanael. We are told too, that, because your father bore the ancient Hebrew name Tholmai, you later came to be known as Bartholomew (the "son of Tholmai").

It was your loyal and devoted friendship for Saint Philip which drew me to you first, Saint Bartholomew—for Saint Philip, I must confess, is a great favorite of mine. (But of course you know what is common gossip—that I've always loved Saint Peter to the point of distraction.) I like the way you clung to Philip all his life, sharing his hardships and joys, unselfishly laboring with him on his missions—and courageously suffering with him at the hands of the executioners who caused his death. Of all his friends, only you, and his sister, Mariamme, were there at the end, tenderly to bury him. During his whole life, you seemed always thus to be thanking him silently for the greatest happiness of your own—your association with the Master. For it was Philip who first brought you to Him. And you never forgot, Saint Bartholomew.

Somehow, of all the Gospel accounts of the several ways in which certain of the Twelve came to Him, the story of your call invokes the most delightful picture. I love to think how you and your friend, Philip, journeyed to Bethania beyond Jordan, to hear that great prophet preach penance to a weary Jewish world, hungry for its long-promised Messiah. There, mingling with the throng which had poured out from all Judea, you must have listened spell-bound to the Baptist's fiery words: "Do penance: for the Kingdom of Heaven is at hand!" And I often wonder how it came about that presently you and Philip separated for a little—certainly you were not together when the Master called him. Frequently have I puzzled over just how you came to be under that fig-tree, Saint Bartholomew! Were you perhaps weary, and had thrown yourself within its shade to rest for a space? Or had you and Philip appointed it as a rendezvous, where you awaited him? Or were you possibly hungry, and so had fallen to plucking the fruit it bore? (I'm very fond of figs myself, Saint Bartholomew —I wish some day that we might enjoy a few together!) Well, anyway, there you were, underneath a lovely fig-tree, when Philip rushed up breathlessly. "We have found," he exclaimed, "Him of Whom . . . the prophets did write—Jesus . . . of Nazareth!"

Now I hope you'll forgive me for reminding you of your reply, for I assure you I realize that very shortly after, you were only too eager to retract it. But poor Philip must have been considerably deflated, when you inquired: "Can anything of good come from Nazareth?" What a question, Saint Bartholomew!

But I'm sure you didn't say it nastily, and that you were sincere, if misguided, in your prejudice against that wonderful little town. Perhaps you'd had some unfortunate experience at the hands of a Nazarene, and thought they all must be exactly alike. Or else you may have been good-naturedly contemptuous of so small a place (you know the way New Yorkers talk about little towns, and it doesn't really mean a thing). Or perhaps your words were uttered in the spirit in which a San Franciscan might refer to Los Angeles—just a display of worthy civic pride.

141

In any case, the question popped out. But your friend was not wasting any time in explanations. "Come and see," he said briefly—and forthwith dragged you off from under the fig-tree. Some distance had to be traversed, before, rounding a bend in the road from which your fig-tree was invisible, you came upon that little group gathered about the Master.

How surprised you must have been, when as you approached, you heard Him exclaim: "Behold an Israelite indeed, in whom there is no guile!" It was a delightful compliment, Saint Bartholomew—but of course you were puzzled by this Stranger's assumption that He knew all about you. "Whence," you demanded, "knowest Thou me?" And then came that amazing reply: "Before that Philip called thee, when thou wast under the fig-tree, I saw thee."

Dear Saint Bartholomew, you were indeed devoid of all guile. You never questioned this statement for a moment, wondering secretly, as others might, whether someone else had actually seen you there, and had told the Master. You simply accepted it—at once more convinced of His power than were others by years of miracles. I've always loved the way you responded. "Rabbi, Thou art the Son of God!", you cried unreservedly. Your heart must have leaped, when

He said gently: "Because I said unto thee, I saw thee under the fig-tree, thou believest: greater things than these shalt thou see. Amen, amen, I say to you, you shall see the heaven opened, and the angels of God ascending and descending upon the Son of Man."

From that first beautifully complete cry of faith, you never thereafter once wavered. Without guile, yes, Saint Bartholomew—but nevertheless, I still insist, not without style. If that lovely white and purple costume is any augury, I'm sure you were the best-dressed Apostle at that famous wedding-party in your native Cana, to which, shortly after your call, you and Philip, Peter, Andrew and John accompanied Him. I'm certain there was no failure on your part, at least, to put on a wedding garment. And there, when you tasted the water miraculously turned to wine, I think perhaps you were even more moved and amazed than the others—because of that old Arabic legend which relates that you were, by occupation, "a dresser of vines, skilled in their cultivation." As such, you would certainly have known your wines like an expert, Saint Bartholomew.

It has often seemed to me that perhaps you were more especially beloved by the Master than were some of the others. For out of all the

143

Twelve, you shared with a chosen few the privilege of being present, not only at that "first beginning of miracles," but also, after the Resurrection, at His tenderly beautiful last appearance on the shores of the Sea of Tiberias. Only five of you were at that wedding-feast—and only seven were fishing when He called to you from the sands. "Children," was the way he hailed you. That scene has always touched me—how, because you were all hungry, He called you in to that sheltered spot where He had prepared hot coals, and a fish, and bread. I think he must always have thought of you particularly as a child, Saint Bartholomew—you, with no guile. And He so loved children. "Unless ye become as one of these"—well, you, for one, had never been otherwise!

Yet the wisdom and valor with which, all your life, you waged your holy war for His cause, were certainly products of a sound maturity. There was nothing childish about that able debate in which you so logically defeated that wily Pharisee on the Temple steps in Jerusalem. In case you have never read how it has been reported, "The Recognitions of Clement" states: "Then a certain Pharisee . . . chid Philip, because he put Jesus on a level with Moses." Now you weren't going to permit anyone to chide your beloved Philip—much less, allow any derogatory remarks about your Master. So: "... to whom, Bartholomew, answering, boldly declared that we do not only say that Jesus was equal to Moses, but that He was greater ... because Moses was indeed a prophet, as Jesus was also, but that Moses was not the Christ, as Jesus was; and therefore He is doubtless greater Who is both prophet and the Christ, than he who is only a prophet."

I've also been much drawn to you, Saint Bartholomew, because of your feminist sympathies, which I can see plainly delineated in that Constitution you wrote, "Concerning the Deaconess". For in your prayer, do you not say: "O Eternal God ... Who didst replenish with the Spirit, Miriam, and Deborah, and Anna, and Huldah; Who didst not disdain that Thy only begotten Son should be born of a woman; Who ... in the Temple, didst ordain women to be keepers of Thy holy gates..."? You didn't want the Lord to forget women, did you, Saint Bartholomew?

And what a traveler you were! For we are told that you preached the Word in Mesopotamia, Persia, Egypt, Armenia, Lycaonia, Phrygia, and even India! Concerning the latter, I should so like to have you reassure me about the truth of that tradition preserved by Eusebius —that there you left with your converts a treasured Hebrew version of the Gospel of Saint Matthew. For it is so pleasant to think that you and Saint Matthew had great sympathy for each other. You see, he liked parties, and—well, you liked clothes (always in saintly moderation, of course) and somehow I think such tastes go together, and should have made you very congenial. I suspect Saint Philip, your most intimate friend, of being quite social, which of course also ties in nicely with your own particular trait. (It's going to be so disappointing if some day I shall have to change all my ideas of you delightful Apostles!)

In the first part of this letter, I questioned you about the veracity of certain remarks, apropos of your clothing, uttered by that pagan god, Becher. But he is credited with other statements concerning you, of whose truth I feel there can be no question. "Seven times a day," he declared, "Bartholomew bends the knee to the Lord, and seven times a night does he pray to God. . . . There go along with him angels of God, who allow him neither to be weary, nor to hunger, nor to thirst; his face and his soul and his heart are always glad and rejoicing." That only confirms my theory that you were, indeed, charming to look upon—for who does not love to gaze into a truly happy face? Especially when it's as handsome as yours!

Poor old Becher—he seemed considerably worried by the thought that you might invade his temple, even as you had invaded Astaruth's, and thus render him equally useless. "I entreat you," he implored his questioners, "if you shall find Bartholomew, entreat him not to come here, lest his angels do to me as they have done to my brother, Astaruth!" But apparently you had plenty of work to keep you occupied in the latter's domain, for it is related that you were so successful there in casting out devils, that you attracted the attention of royalty. You perhaps haven't forgotten that King Polymius had a daughter possessed of such, and that he besought you to cure her. As you may recall, you accomplished this easily; but I note from the account that you spurned the camels he sent you, laden "with gold and silver, precious stones, pearls, and"—what's this? Yes, it says so very plainly: "clothing"! Perhaps I'd best retract some of my former statements, Saint Bartholomew—especially in view of your reprimand to the King. "For these gifts those persons long, who seek earthly things," you said very definitely.

How much I admire the neat way in which

you finally converted King Polymius and his entire realm! It couldn't have been more convincing. Of course you knew, without any sense of vanity, how easily men were affected by appearances—and it must have been with this thought in mind that you staged that little drama. You remember how you invited them all into the temple, to witness the final overthrow of the demon who had been, for all those years, masquerading as their god, Astaruth. It must have been thrilling when you called upon him to come forth from that graven image, and reveal himself in his true colors. It was the devastating contrast that did it, I'm sure, Saint Bartholomew. For there you stood, in that stunning white and purple costume, your handsome face exalted by prayer—when out came Mr. Demon. And he was, the account states, "black as soot, his face sharp like a dog's, thin-cheeked, with hair down to his feet, eyes like fire, sparks coming out of his mouth, and out of his nostrils came forth smoke like sulphur; with wings spined like a porcupine"! To say the least, he could not have looked pretty, as he "flew away, groaning and weeping". Of course those people took one look at you both, and decided there was no argument. You must have been very happy as you baptized them all—and what a triumph, when the King

"laid aside his diadem, and followed Bartholomew, the Apostle of Christ"! When he became
such an ardent and holy Christian that you felt
justified in making him a bishop, your joy must
indeed have been great.

It was a shocking thing, Saint Bartholomew,
that two members of the same family could have
been so totally different. For was it not Polymius's own brother, King Astyages, monarch of
Albanopolis, who refused not only to be converted, but was so enraged over your success with
Polymius, that he "rent the purple in which he
was clothed"? To see him thus wilfully destroy-
ing his clothing must have greatly distressed you,
who took such good care of your own! I
could forgive him if only he had let his rage end
there—and not had you scourged and tortured,
and finally condemned you to die. Poor Saint
Bartholomew, this was how he rewarded you
for having brought only gentleness and beauty
and healing to his people! But you did not falter
—for indeed you were an old hand at such situ-
ations, having once before, with Saint Philip in
Phrygia, received the death sentence, and been
actually nailed fast to the gates of a pagan temple. True, you had at length been released by the
eleventh-hour repentance of your captors—but
you must have fallen into their arms more dead

than alive. And it seems likely that when this second condemnation came, years after, you still bore the scars of that dreadful experience.

This time you knew there was to be no release —yet that did not prevent you, as you were dying, from preaching the Risen Christ any less earnestly. And I feel sure, when your last suffering moment came, that your face was even more than ever "glad and rejoicing". For you were giving your life for Him in Whose service you had labored so long, so lovingly, and so well.

If I ever should have the happiness of meeting you, Saint Bartholomew, perhaps you will tell me just which method that cruel king used in accomplishing your death. For some reports say that he had you beheaded, and others that you were crucified, and still others that you were flayed alive. In any case, I'm sure those paintings inspired by the latter theory, must ever have been distasteful to you—for they represent you as flayed, and holding in your hands, your own skin. Personally, they distress me greatly, not only because of the pain and horror I feel at imagining such terrible suffering—but also because I do not think this quite the proper way to depict one who was always so well-dressed.

I for one love to see you only in that spotlessly white garment and cloak bordered with purple—your beautiful eyes searching into the souls of men, and your handsome head held valiantly high in His service, no matter what the peril. For you see, even though it be a weakness, there are some of us who do like our Apostles well-dressed. For such, what could be pleasanter than to think of you as always, without guile, to be sure—but yet with just lots of style, Saint Bartholomew!

IN JUSTICE TO
SAINT JAMES THE JUST

IN JUSTICE TO
SAINT JAMES THE JUST

M<small>Y</small> plans were completed to make public an apologia of you, Saint James—kinsman of the Lord, and first Bishop of Jerusalem —which would bear the caption, "In Justice to Saint James the Just". But at the very moment of releasing it the title itself gave me pause. Happily it occurred to me in time that the most honest manner of living up to such a title would be the private submission of my ideas to you first. Not that I particularly want to submit them; for while I've always longed to establish some sort of personal communication with you, yet something tells me this is going about it in the worst possible way.

For such an apologia would, frankly, be written to give you some publicity (for which, in my unworthy opinion, you have long been suffering) but yet there was not one of the Apostles who shrank from publicity as much as you! If you don't throw it in the wastebasket immediately, I know what you'll do to this synopsis— you'll blue-pencil practically every line. But couldn't you bring yourself to amend its more flagrant passages, and mark it "o.k. with corrections"? That would be ever so nice of you, Saint James.

Yet it is so discouragingly apparent that, while on earth at least, you despised any form of notoriety. I really feel like being a little severe with you about this, for while perhaps one of the most estimable qualities of sainthood, still it can result in the public's being woefully misinformed, leading to no end of injustice to perfectly wonderful persons—like yourself, for instance.

Just look what it has led to in your case. Simply because you were so modest as to write, at the beginning of that beautiful Epistle: "James, the servant of God, and of Our Lord, Jesus Christ," instead of putting it plainly: "James, the servant of God, and *kinsman* of Our Lord, Jesus Christ," there have been thousands who have denied that you, the author of that Epistle, were also one of "the brethren [cousins] of the Lord". You simply could not bring yourself to put down in black and white, the fact that you were related, by blood, to your Master. That you held that particularly precious and glorious honor, you humbly confessed to yourself, was no doing of yours; and therefore, unlike,

156

let us say, our Mayflower descendants, you wouldn't go boasting about your genealogy.

Yet many of those blunt-minded critics, who insist your omission to mention the fact conclusively proves that you were not related to the Saviour, agree however that the author of that Epistle was the first bishop of Jerusalem—another fact to which you make no reference. It's inconsistent of them to think that because in that epistolary greeting you didn't dub yourself a kinsman of the Lord, you were not—and at the same time to think that you were, though not so styling yourself, Bishop of Jerusalem! Even as you were too modest to claim a relationship to your Lord, so were you too modest to refer to your high ecclesiastical position in the early Church. But I really think it would have been better for all concerned, had you not been such a shrinking violet, and had come out flatfootedly with the truth. It would have saved endless and bitter argument among the theologians—but I suppose you will tell me that it would thus have worked a great hardship. There would have been nothing to argue, concerning you. Perhaps you were wise, after all, Saint James.

Nevertheless, the fact remains that scant justice has been done you—you who, of all the Twelve, won the greatest renown in doing justice to others. For were you not known, even to your enemies, as "James the Just"? Of course the appellation embraced more than merely a fair attitude toward your fellow-men—it also carried the greater implication of a just life in the sense of a holy and virtuous one. It is a beautiful title, Saint James—and I, for one, recoil when I see it disregarded, and allusion made to you by that other cognomen, by which unhappily you were also known—"James the Less". Scholars aver that the latter was given you solely because of your shortness of stature, and to distinguish you from that other Apostle, James, the son of Zebedee. Because, in your stocking-feet, so to speak, you stood several inches short of him, some reprehensible person christened you James the Less—and thus was guilty of a deplorable injustice. For generations have taken this title to indicate that you were a negligible quantity among the Twelve! The truth is that you were one of the greatest. For this reason, I do wish that you could bring yourself to countenance a little publicity, Saint James!

The first thing I would like to make clear in that apologia, for instance, would be your parentage—that you were the son of Alpheus (sometimes called Cleophas) and Mary, the sister of the Mother of Jesus. It has bothered a good many that there could have been two sisters in the same family named Mary—but we have the word of no less an early authority than Papias (and later, Saint Jerome) that such was the case. I should like to explain how you and your brothers, Joses, Simon, and Jude, were cousins of Our Lord, and called in the Gospels, His "brethren" —a term then applied in Judea to all near kinsmen. It may strike you as bromidic, but nevertheless, because it's good publicity, I would also mention the fact that, like all great men, you had a great mother. She was of the stuff of courage and loyalty; for Saint John relates: "Now there stood by the cross of Jesus, His mother, and His mother's sister, Mary [wife] of Cleophas, and Mary Magdalen." And Saint Mark recounts that after your Lord's burial, "when the Sabbath was past, Mary Magdalen, and Mary the mother of James, and Salome, bought sweet spices, that coming, they might anoint Jesus." These three women remained with Him unto death, and after—fearing neither the Jews, nor the Roman soldiers, nor even the sepulchre itself, into which they entered that first Easter morn. To them goes the glory of being the first to know that their Lord had truly risen. If this apologia is ever written, Saint James, I promise you that I shall generously silence all personal feminist persuasions and refrain from bringing up the question: when His mother, and your mother, and Mary Magdalen were all at the foot of the cross—where (with the exception of Saint John) were all you men? Yet you'd do me a great favor if you'd quietly take Saint Paul aside, and call his attention to the fact that at that place of grief and peril the women outnumbered the men, three to one.

I think, also, that it would be best if I refrained from dwelling upon your early attitude toward your Lord, which was not, it would seem, as replete with faith as it later became. There might be some who would not understand— though I hasten to add that I do, Saint James. For it must have been difficult at first, because of your close relationship to the Saviour, with Whom, no doubt, you and your brothers had played familiarly as children, and Whose everyday life was so like your own, to believe this Cousin was, in truth, the long-awaited Messiah. It was natural that you could not accept this fact as quickly as those to whom He was a comparative stranger. He Himself declared: "A prophet is not without honour, but in his own country, and in his own house, and among his own kindred." So it was that, even after He had wrought many miracles, you cousins still had your doubts—and accordingly behaved as cousins naturally would! Mischievously, you'd put Him to the test, you and your brothers. For when "He would not walk in Judea . . . His brethren said to Him . . . 'Go into Judea, that Thy disciples also may see Thy works . . . for there is no man that doth anything in secret, and he himself seeketh to be known openly. If Thou do these things, manifest Thyself to the world.' For," continues Saint John, "neither did His brethren believe in Him." Slow to convince, yet when at last convinced, what a staunch faith you had, Saint James! Yours is a superb story—please don't be cross with me for wanting to recount it once more.

This early scepticism, then, was only after all "cousinly," on the part of you and your brothers—yet the Beloved Master, unlike, indeed, any ordinary cousin, did not hold these first qualms against you. Having seen faith at length flower in your hearts, when He came down from the mountain after that long night of prayer and calling His followers to Him, appointed the Twelve who were thereafter to be His closest companions, He chose for that select group at least two of His own kinsmen—you and your brother, Saint Jude. Many have thought that He also chose another of your brothers, Simon. Certain it is that the Twelve included a Simon, besides Simon-Peter.

We know that you, Saint James, gladly followed Him from that day; and that, even though you did not play a leading rôle in those brief, joy-laden, sorrow-laden years of His ministry, yet after His death you were among the ablest and most active in spreading His gospel. Of all His cousins, you were perhaps the dearest to Him—for after His Resurrection it is related that He once appeared especially to you alone. Saint Paul mentions the fact, and Saint Jerome has preserved its lovely story. He recounts that you had taken a solemn vow not to eat bread, from the time that you had "drunk the cup of the Lord," until you should "see Him risen from among them that sleep." Shortly before His Ascension, He came to you as you sat grieving alone. " 'Bring,' saith the Lord, 'a table and bread.' He took bread, and blessed it, and brake it, and then gave it to James the Just, and said to him: 'My brother, eat thy bread, for the Son of Man is risen from among them that sleep.' "

He would not have you go hungry for long. I'd like more people to realize, Saint James, that not only were you most dear to Him, but also that you were greatly beloved by your fellow-Apostles. Their affection for you—their respect for the strict and careful religious training in which you had been reared—led them to make you the apostolic head of the Jerusalem Church. Eusebius writes that "Peter and James [son of Zebedee] and John, after the . . . Resurrection, though preëminently honoured by the Lord, did not contend for glory, but made James the Just, bishop of Jerusalem." As between friends, Saint James, the job they gave you could not have been any bed of roses! Yet you administered it superbly. I am thinking of the delicate diplomacy and sturdy courage you were called upon to display on many an occasion. There was that time, for instance, when militant Paul, whom you knew only as a ruthless persecutor of Christians, suddenly announced his conversion and came to see you. Didn't you quiver in your boots until it became plain that he was actually sincere? And that time when, later, he aroused all sorts of controversy within the fold, by releasing his Gentile converts from observance of certain Jewish religious rites which the more conservative disciples considered a definite prerequisite of Christianity. At the council you called to argue that question, your position as arbiter could have been no easy one—yet you settled the matter so fairly that no man could object. Your word was loved, and your disapproval feared, by all Christians—and you governed that first flock with such administrative wisdom as to be a model for all future bishops. To those who, far afield, were preaching the Gospel, and who sought your sanction on all they did, you tirelessly sent emissaries and instructions. Ignatius, of the first century, in his Epistle to the Trallians, states that you were assisted in your vast work by Saint Stephen, whom you appointed deacon. But the Jews had to go and stone your deacon to death; and I feel sure, poor Saint James, that you never quite got over this loss.

In my contemplated apologia, I should like to quote (but of course not without your approval) from that ancient Syriac document, "The Teaching of the Apostles," which says: "Jerusalem received the ordination to the priesthood, as did all the country of Palestine, and the parts occupied by the Samaritans and the parts occupied by the Philistines, and the country of the Arabians, and of Phoenicia, and the people of Caesaria, from James, who was ruler and guide in the Church of the Apostles."

If your modesty would allow me to go this far, it would only be a small step further to permit me to trespass on more personal ground—though I confess its tactful introduction to you seems a rather ticklish matter. But it would be such a good point, if you would only allow me to repeat the words of Hegesippus regarding your habits! After all, you didn't prevent him writing, in the second century, about them—and merely because I am more polite, and am asking your permission first, I don't see why you should rob me of this splendid "copy": "James the Just drank no wine or other intoxicating liquor, nor did he eat flesh; no razor came upon his head; he did not anoint himself with oil, nor make use of the bath." In these times, when people are so reluctant to give up physical luxuries, I think they should be reminded just what a holy ascetic you voluntarily were, Saint James. To be sure, some of the more godless might find fault with you—first of all, on the liquor question. But I could easily silence those who might criticize your teetotalism, by quoting your own words regarding this matter as it pertained to others. No fanatical "dry" were you. You might prefer to abstain completely—but you did not exact your followers to do likewise. For in "The Constitution of James," which is part of the patristic literature of the Church, you wrote:

"Now the Scripture says: '...let them not drink wine, lest by drinking, they forget wisdom and are not able to judge aright.' ...We say... not that they are not to drink at all, otherwise it would be to the reproach of what God has made for cheerfulness, but that they be not disordered with wine." And though you were by choice a vegetarian, I'm sure you allowed others perfect freedom in this regard. As for the whiskers, if you preferred them on yourself, that was your own business. Certainly, the most eminent of the Victorians also cultivated them assiduously, and why should the twentieth century consider itself more enlightened on this subject? Some of the same godless critics might here try to quote your own Epistle to our confusion: "For if a man be ... not a doer, he shall be compared to a man beholding his own countenance in a glass. For he beheld himself, and went his way —and presently forgot what manner of man he was." They might say this is exactly what you did, since no razor "ever came upon your head" —and that if you had remembered what manner of man you were, you certainly would have shaved. But they are such a prejudiced lot, it wouldn't be worth our while to pay any attention.

If you could only bring yourself to submit to the notoriety, the further words of Hegesippus would be an inspiration to a world which has begun to find its only sure solace in prayer. "James," he continued, "was wont to go to the

Temple, and he used to be found kneeling on his knees, begging forgiveness for the people, so that the skin of his knees became horny like that of a camel's." Poor Saint James! It must have hurt a lot, before it became horny—the stones of the Temple—well, they were stones! You spent so many hours in prayer, you administered your see so competently, and you wrote so much, that I suspect you never got any sleep. For besides your wonderful Epistle, you wrote "constitutions" on all sorts of matters, ranging from virginity ("this is a state of voluntary trial, not for the reproach of marriage, but on account of leisure for piety") to evening prayer. And finally you compiled a liturgy of the Mass. It is putting it mildly to say that few bishops have been as active.

You may have shunned publicity for yourself, but when it came to giving it to your Master, you were ready in truth to shout it from the housetops—or, to be exact, from the steps of the Temple; and finally, from its very pinnacle! That this required reckless courage, I should very much like to emphasize in the apologia, if you don't mind. You perhaps have not even yet forgotten that time when you were preaching your Lord's gospel from the Temple steps, and the Jews began to heckle you. "The Recognitions of Clement" explains that your bold words infuriated the unbelievers in the crowd and that a great tumult finally ensued. But they could not quiet you. Then, says Clement, "some one of our enemies . . . seizing a strong brand from the altar, set the example of smiting . . . And that enemy attacked James and threw him headlong from the top of the steps; and supposing him to be dead, he cared not to inflict further violence upon him. But our friends lifted him up . . . and we returned to the house of James, and spent the night there in prayer." I hope, in your modesty, that you did not scold Saint Peter, for giving publicity to your sufferings on that occasion. Personally, I think he did just the right thing in spreading the story. But perhaps you never saw that letter he wrote in the course of a journey upon which you'd sent him. In it he recounted how he had stopped at the home of Zacchaeus, a Christian living some distance from Jerusalem, who had inquired solicitously of Peter after your own health. "I told him," wrote Peter, "that James was still lame in one foot . . . I related how James, standing on the top of the steps, had for seven successive days shown the whole people from the Scriptures . . . that Jesus is the Christ." And what was being hurled headlong down those hard, marble steps—what was a painful, lame foot to you—as long as there were some in that savage crowd who had opened their hearts to your message?

When I think of your own gentle, peace-loving nature, I am distressed that circumstances more than once made you the victim of such violent scenes. Poor Saint James! No wonder you wrote, concerning evening prayer: "Let us beg of the Lord . . . for the angel of peace . . . for an evening and a night of peace." To be sure, you closed with a petition that lay even deeper in your heart. "And let us," you wrote, "beg that the whole course of our life may be unblameable!"

In your exquisite Epistle, you unconsciously gave a more accurate account of your own lovely character than can ever be penned by any rash blunderer such as I. You pled with your flock to practise patience—"My dearest brethren, let every man be swift to hear, but slow to speak, and slow to anger." You begged them to be un-wavering in faith. You told them that "a double-minded man is inconstant in all his ways," and besought such to purify their hearts. You up-braided them for "dishonouring the poor man," and for reverencing the rich. You reminded them that the tongue was "an unquiet evil, full of deadly poison," and you bade them "swear not . . . but let your speech be, yea, yea; no, no."

And I love that part where you wrote: "Is any of you sad? Let him pray.—Is he cheerful in mind? Let him sing!" As frequently as they have been quoted, I should not be able, in my apologia, to refrain from once more repeating your beautiful words: "Every best gift, and every perfect gift, is from above, coming down from the Father of Lights, with Whom there is no change, nor shadow of alteration." But I think you have summed up your own nature most completely in the lines: "The wisdom that is from above, first indeed is chaste; then peaceable; modest; easy to be persuaded; consenting to the good; full of mercy and good fruits; without judging; without dissimulation. And the fruit of justice is sown in peace, to them that make peace. . . . Religion clean and undefiled before God and the Father, is this: to visit the fatherless and the widows in their tribulation; and to keep one's self unspotted from this world."

Such was your own life, dear, gentle Saint James—and it is no wonder that in that stormy, turbulent Jerusalem even the most fanatical unbelievers revered you. In fact, the just life you led was so admired, in spite of your modesty, that it was indirectly the cause of your death. Greater and greater had grown the number of your converts. "Those who did believe, believed because of James," wrote Hegesippus, "...and when many even of the ruling class believed, there was a commotion among the Jews." To quiet it, he recounts that the Scribes and Pharisees came to you, saying: "For we all listen to thy persuasion, since we, as well as all the people, bear thee testimony that thou art just, and showest partiality to none." I imagine that this, as any praise, annoyed you, who wished truly to seem least among the children of men. No doubt you were troubled when Hegesippus wrote down so meticulously the ensuing events—how these same Pharisees besought you to quiet the people, assembled from all Judea for the observance of the Passover, by climbing to the summit of the Temple and publicly pronouncing that Jesus was not the Christ. And how therein you saw a great opportunity—though not exactly the one the Pharisees had in mind! You agreed to mount to that lofty pinnacle, and once there, as you recall, you proceeded to startle your solicitors by loudly proclaiming to the multitude that in truth, Jesus *was* the Christ. The historian recounts that they cried in dismay, " 'Oh, oh, the Just Man himself is in error!' So they went up and threw down the Just Man, and said to one another: 'Let us stone James the Just!' And they began to stone him, for he was not killed by the fall; but he turned and kneeled down, and said: 'I beseech Thee, Lord God, our Father, forgive them.' ... But one among them, one of the fullers, took the staff with which he was accustomed to wring out the garments he dyed, and hurled it at the head of the Just Man. And so he suffered martyrdom."

Not only did Hegesippus thus publish your story to the world, but Josephus, in the eighteenth book of his "Antiquities of the Jews," went even further in treading on your sensibilities by alleging that the total destruction of Jerusalem, which followed soon after your death, was directly due to your martyrdom—a punishment on the city for the cruelty it had inflicted upon its greatest citizen.

In view of what these two famous historians have written, without the slightest regard for your preference for privacy, I don't see how, Saint James, you can find it in your heart to forbid me to write the apologia I have planned —especially since I have been polite enough to submit its outline to you first. For remember, you were, and always will be, "James the Just". Do I hear you say that there are limits to justice? Well, then, please think of this, Saint James— the truly great cannot escape publicity, even from the unworthiest sources. So don't you think you had better submit quietly to the inevitable?

WERE YOU BROTHERS, SAINT SIMON AND SAINT JUDE?

WERE YOU BROTHERS,
SAINT SIMON AND
SAINT JUDE?

D EAR Saint Simon and Saint Jude:
You will not, I trust, be offended when
I address you thus jointly, being as you are so
accustomed to that sort of thing. Though I've
often wondered if sometimes it hasn't gotten a
bit on your nerves—this constant coupling of
your names since the earliest Christian centuries.
Not that I've ever doubted your sincere pleasure
in each other's society—only occasionally this
double-harness must have been somewhat trying
to your more individualistic tendencies.

As you know, the western church, for instance, has only begrudgingly allotted you one
feast-day between you—October twenty-eighth
—so I'm sure you must have appreciated it when
the eastern church generously gave you one
apiece.

Inseparable though you have been in the
minds of men, and even though sharing much
in common, I see you each as very distinct personalities. Both among that choice group of

Twelve whom He called to leave all things and follow Him, you must have experienced from the first a close kinship in spiritual ideals—and many have thought that you shared the closer kinship of physical relationship. In fact that matter has puzzled me so greatly that it is why I am writing to you. I see no way toward any peace of mind on the subject, unless I ask you outright. In fine, I would know, if you would be so kind as to tell me, whether you two are brothers—and hence, both actual cousins of your Lord. For it is very plain that you, Saint Jude, were His cousin, sharing with your brother, Saint James the Just, that signally glorious honor. It is also clear that you had another brother who was named Simon. Now you, Saint Simon, we know as the Apostle—but nowhere is your identity definitely merged with that Simon who was a brother of Saint Jude. Yet it would be ever so pleasant, if it were—for that would mean that three of His cousins were among the Twelve. I should like to think this was so, because we are told at the first: "neither did His brethren [cousins] believe in Him," and it would be so comforting to think that at least three of them had later made amends for this earlier slight, by laboring only as Apostles could labor, in His cause.

But of all the Apostles, you, Saint Simon,

seem the most reluctant to be known—except perhaps Saint James the Just, who was always hiding his head under a bushel. Because you both so shunned publicity, makes it seem very probable indeed, that you really were, with Saint Jude, brothers. Your very reticence makes me suspect you of being one of the greatest of the Twelve. For had He not said:—"He that is the greater among you, let him become as the younger; and he that is the leader, as he that serveth"?—It would seem as though you particularly had taken these words to heart, so humble a part do you play in the Gospel record, where only your name is mentioned as one of the Apostles.

And indeed, I agree with you, Saint Simon— that this in itself was sufficient honor to satisfy any man!

Perhaps it even amused you, when you saw the Evangelists trying so carefully to give you a distinct individuality. I can almost hear you saying, "What do I care?" when they so meticulously endeavored to distinguish you from Simon-Peter —Matthew and Mark by calling you "Simon, the Cananean"—and Luke, by the words, "Simon who is called Zelotes." And I expect you turned away in sheer boredom when you witnessed the endless controversies waging here below, on whether "the Cananean" meant a resident of

Cana—or whether "Zelotes" meant you were a member of that fiercely patriotic Jewish party, the Zealots—or whether (as now seems to be accepted) both "Kananites" (the Cananean) and Zelotes really mean exactly the same thing, being translations of the Hebrew word for "zealous." Personally, that view satisfies me—for I'm sure, especially if you were brother to Saint James the Just, and Saint Jude—that you were indeed zealous—first in strictly observing the Jewish law which you had learned from childhood in that extremely pious family; and later, in as strictly following the law of love which He had laid down for His followers.

The Zealots, I understand, were in a sense revolutionists—plotting and scheming and fighting relentlessly, to free their beloved Judea from the yoke of imperial Rome. Now somehow I can't picture you as belligerent enough to be one of them—at least, not after you had heard Him discourse on the necessity of "turning the other cheek."

As quiet and unobtrusive as you were, however, you never shirked your duties as an Apostle. Though I can imagine it was painful for you to have to appear in public that time, when it fell to your lot to debate on the Temple steps with that disciple of John the Baptist, who misguidedly insisted that John was the Messiah. Your modesty did not prevent you from most capably refuting all his arguments. But when he at last subsided, I suspect you sighed gratefully: "I'm glad that's over!" And that you got out of sight as quickly as possible.

I think also that you must have been a stickler for form, because you left those two carefully-written constitutions—concerning the ordination of bishops, and the duties of all church officials—both very specific and definite in their details.

In your self-effacing efforts to keep future Christianity from sticking its nose into your personal business there was at least one matter you were not able to cover up successfully—and that was your propensity for travel! For all the authorities agree that you were a great globetrotter, and that you preached His gospel in practically every known country of your contemporary world. And even though I know you hate to be bothered, Saint Simon, I do wish, in addition to the matter of your kinship to Saint Jude, that you would clear up for me the question of that "island in the West" which you are said to have visited. For some claim that it was really Britain—which was indeed, "a long way from home"; but, with your fondness for travel, I can imagine you accomplishing such a journey with the greatest nonchalance.

Though all know that you were martyred after a long life spent laboring for Him—still nobody seems to know exactly where! I suppose you are just as glad—though it must have been annoying to have alleged relics of you turn up all over—scattered in utter abandonment from Babylon even to France and Italy. Now as long as I have the temerity to ask you those other questions, I don't see why I shouldn't ask you to tell me just where you died. If you wish, I shall treat it as confidential—only I can't help wondering whether it was really in Persia, at Suanir, as the Latins claim; or in Weriosphora in Iberia, as Moses of Chorene would have it; or in Jerusalem or Britain as still others maintain.

The one thing about you that greatly distresses me, Saint Simon, is that gruesome implement, the saw! For I have been taught to search for it as your symbol in Christian art—all because of the tradition that, wherever you did meet your death, you were sawed to pieces! I think that was horrible—and, if true, I can't see why they must be perpetually reminding you of such unspeakable torture by forever painting that old saw beside you. But if you really were sawed to pieces, as unpleasant as the thought is,

I suppose it's not strange, after all, that relics of you have turned up all over the world.

One thing more—you have always been so favorably disposed to tanners, who long ago made you their patron-saint. Now is this because perhaps you yourself were by profession a tanner? It certainly is a useful trade, and, if you were, I can imagine that you were a very valuable member of that little company—for the Twelve must have needed leather-goods more than most people. They were all such inveterate travelers, and must have been very hard on their sandals and satchels.

Now, Saint Jude, I hope all these questions addressed to Saint Simon have not wearied you. If you really are his brother, I'm sure you haven't minded. And I hasten to implore you not to take it as a personal slight, that of you two, I am not only addressing you last, but am also writing you last of all the Apostles. For I assure you, not for nothing have I purposely left you till the end. I have most sound and cogent reasons, with which I am sure you will sympathize when I explain—which I shall do anon.

But first let me tell you how glad I am, that you at least, made your relationship to Saint James the Just, and hence, to your Lord, very clear.—In the salutation of that Epistle which

181

you have left us, addressed to the early Church, you specifically state: "Jude, the servant of Jesus Christ, and brother of James: To them that are beloved in God the Father, and preserved in Jesus Christ, and called."

Now although you, even as James in his Epistle, take pains to say "the servant of Jesus Christ," instead of the "servant and *kinsman* of Jesus Christ"—I know, as with your brother, that this omission was prompted only by modesty and humility. The fact that I've sometimes thought that all you Apostles went to exaggerated lengths in cultivating these two virtues, is only a woeful comment on me—and on the great chasm that lies between the Apostolic age, and the advertising age, of which, alas, I am a product. None of you dear people ever believed in blowing your own horn—you left that to Gabriel, as the only one with a perfect right to do so.

Humility marked your family, if it ever marked any; and it was a humility that nothing could disturb. For even though the distinguished honor of the first bishopric of Jerusalem was bestowed upon your brother, James, it didn't turn his head in the slightest. Your parents, Alpheus and Mary, had certainly given their sons a thoroughly religious training—and one that fitted you perfectly, when He called you, to be His Apostles.

They had, it would seem, particularly dedicated you to the religious life, even when they named you—calling you Jude-Thaddeus, the latter signifying in Syriac, one who was to praise God. Both names are beautiful; and it has always seemed to me a great pity that one other of His chosen Twelve, should have borne a name so closely approximating yours—Judas Iscariot. I have observed how the Evangelists, Saint Matthew and Saint Mark, in their desire not to confuse your identity with his, have referred to you in the list of the Apostles, merely by your last name—Thaddeus; and how Saint Luke has gotten around the difficulty by calling you, "Jude, the brother of James."

I've often wondered how you like the translation of your name into "Lebbaeus"—which, I've been told, appears in the Greek text of Saint Matthew's Gospel, being the word in that tongue for one who praised God.

Humble as you were, I'm sure you weren't in the least hurt, when only Saint John, of all the Evangelists, quoted your comment at the Last Supper. It seems to me, from the question you then put, Saint Jude, that your noticeable lack of self-pride was only equalled—and even excelled

—by your pride in Him. You cannot have forgotten how He said, in that last beautiful discourse: "He that loveth Me, shall be loved of My Father: and I will love him, and will manifest Myself to him." That was all right, you thought —only it might exclude a great many people. And as your Lord and your God, you wanted the whole world to witness His glory! That must have been why you asked: "Lord, how is it that Thou wilt manifest Thyself to us, and not to the world?" I think, Saint Jude, that you may even have pouted a little as you said this.

But the Master made it very clear that He would only "abide" in those who loved Him and kept His word—and you had to be satisfied with that, as small an audience as it provided.

But I like the way you made up your mind that you would always do your part, at least, in spreading the news of His glory. For this cause it is said that you not only carried those tidings to all Judea and Samaria, but also to such distant places as Idumæa, Armenia, Syria, Persia, Mesopotamia, and Libya. And to make that news more enduring, you supplemented the spoken word, with the written, in your Epistle to the Jewish converts. Origen declares that it "contains strong doctrine in a few lines," and while I am no Origen, I can see that for myself. You implored your followers not to be swayed by certain deplorable heresies which had recently arisen; and to hate "the spotted garment which is carnal." But there are two other things about that Epistle which please me even more than these, Saint Jude. One of them is that I seem to see, in your concluding paragraph, the same persistent thought which lay at the root of your question at the Last Supper. If He would not manifest His glory to the whole world, you at least would speak your piece about it: "To the only God, our Saviour, through Jesus Christ Our Lord, be glory and magnificence, empire and power, before all ages, and now, and for all ages of ages, Amen." That was how you felt about it —and you would tell the world!

To be sure, the other thing that pleases me so about your Epistle, arises only from that singularly personal peculiarity of mine—my totally abandoned partiality for Saint Peter. For scholars have noted that you use many expressions in your letter which Saint Peter had written in his own Epistles some years earlier. It simply delights me that you had read him and admired him to this extent. That thought alone makes me sure that you and I would be truly sympathetic, Saint Jude. And I, for one, think it's too bad that there was also a disciple—one of the seventy-two

—who was named Thaddeus. Because while I'm sure he was a very holy man, still it's distressing to note, because you each bore the same name, how he is constantly getting the credit for having done wonderful things which my fondness for you convinces me should be yours.

I sympathize with you, too, because you were a married man and a martyr. Not that the one necessarily made you the other—only that the former must have sometimes conflicted with your work as an Apostle—and the latter, while winning you that incorruptible crown, still must have caused you very great physical suffering. We know that you were married because two of your grandsons (or so Eusebius quotes Hegesippus) lived until the reign of Trajan. I'm sure you made them a perfectly charming grandfather, Saint Jude. As for your martyrdom, I'd be so obliged to you, if you would tell me just where it occurred—whether in Persia, as some say, or in Armenia, as others claim. It must have been just agonizing torture to be made the target for all those arrows which rained steadily upon you until they accomplished your death upon that cross.

And now do you remember how I said in the beginning of this missive, that I had my own good reasons for addressing you last of all the

Apostles? You see, I knew from the start, that, after I had written letters to all the others, I would particularly need your aid. For, as you realize, you are preëminently known to mankind as the "Helper in Cases Despaired-of". Never too desperate the cause for you to undertake—so runs your reputation here below. Dear Saint Jude, it is because you have always responded so graciously when addressed as "Help of the Hopeless" that I now appeal to you. For indeed, I am well nigh hopeless, when I contemplate what I have done! Won't you please take up my case with the other Apostles, upon whom I have rashly inflicted these letters—and beg them not to be too hard on me? Some of them may, and with good reason perhaps, wish to sue me for libel—but I'm sure, if you'll explain to them how truly devoted I am to all of you, everything will be all right between us.

TO SAINT MARK—
CONCERNING
THE PURSE-BEARER

TO SAINT MARK—
CONCERNING
THE PURSE-BEARER

ALTHOUGH usually not in the least backward about writing letters—in fact, quite alarmingly otherwise—I nevertheless, Saint Mark, undertake this particular missive in fear and hesitancy. Not, I hasten to add, because it's addressed to you; for always admiring you greatly I have long since been soothed by the delusion that we are actually very old and intimate friends, you and I. (I hope you don't mind.)

But the questions I would ask you in this letter are so fraught with the quivering breath of tragedy, that my hand falters as I write, and gladly would I lay down my pen and follow the sunshine whose golden song calls to me through the open windows. Alas, that yet so many times heretofore have I allowed it to win me away from this task—although with all its fascination it has never succeeded in completely silencing the aching necessity within my soul persistently decreeing that some day, sometime, this letter must be written.

The pity of it is, I am so fond of you that I would not, for anything in the world, harass you —yet harass you this missive surely must. Nor, as much as I should like to spare you, can I bring myself to indite it to any but you. So, at the very start, I would beg your forgiveness, and implore your help, Saint Mark.

Have you not guessed by now that this letter would seek information about the twelfth of that little company whom He chose, on that long-ago time, to be His special and privileged companions? In fine, it is concerning the man of Kerioth —Judas—that I write you.

Do not turn away, I beg you. It is true that you might well find excuse for doing so in the reason that there are indeed others of whom I might more properly inquire. One of the Twelve, for instance, who were his comrades daily during those three wondrous years of the Master's ministry on earth. For of course I realize, Saint Mark, that you came to labor for His cause only after His death—and knew His chosen Apostles intimately only after their number had been depleted by one—Judas himself. You had not the good fortune to be one of that first holy cohort —yet it is lovely to reflect how your Lord saw to it that you should have, in a way, compensations for not being included in that specially chosen group. Next best to that was the great privilege you held in being a close friend, a loving pupil, of the leader of that group—of dear Saint Peter.

It was from him, we are told, that you learned all the lessons the Master had taught His Apostles before He was stretched upon that dark cross of Calvary. It is charming to think of you eagerly drinking in those lessons, and of Saint Peter as eagerly instructing you, until at length you were recognized as such an authority upon them that the brethren importuned you to write them all down in an enduring record. I have always been grateful to those "brethren," whose names we do not even know—save for them, we should have no beautiful Gospel of Saint Mark.

"Mark, the disciple and interpreter of Peter, himself also handed down to us in writing what was preached by Peter," wrote Saint Irenæus. And for the sake of all Christendom, I'm so glad you did, Saint Mark!

But I yet haven't said why I have selected you to be my informant in this timorous quest for the truth about Judas. To be sure, during your life you never knew him personally—but I rather believe your beloved teacher, Saint Peter, knew him better than did any other of the Twelve; for Peter was, in a sense, father to them all. Yet somehow I cannot bring myself to write

Saint Peter about Judas. No topic I might select could be as tragic—and I simply cannot bear to make Saint Peter sad. He had so much sorrow during his life, his tears fell so constantly in repentance for his unfortunate denial, that I do not want him now to have to think upon "old, unhappy, far-off things" any more than is necessary. Forgive me, dear Saint Mark, for preferring rather to distress you. But surely, next to Peter himself, there is no one better equipped to tell me the whole story. Many and long and intimate must have been the talks you two had together (I could almost be jealous of you, Saint Mark, if you weren't such a very nice person) and we know how tenderly Peter felt toward you from what he wrote in his first Epistle. "The church that is in Babylon . . . saluteth you: and so doth my son Mark." Of course he must have told you more about Judas than you ever set down in your Gospel.

If you will only hear me out, I promise to put my questions as briefly as I can. Didn't Saint Peter ever tell you, for instance, something more of the early life—the family background—of Judas, than is recorded in the New Testament? Now perhaps, even if we knew more about him, his story would seem just as baffling—yet because so little is told, each succeeding Christian generation has puzzled over his psychology as the most incomprehensible enigma presented in all history. You can see, I'm sure, Saint Mark, how difficult it has been for us to understand how one alone, out of Twelve especially selected by the Master, who had shared with the others the sanctification of that Holy Presence through all those years, could have, in the end, so blackly turned traitor to his God.

When such an irrational action occurs nowadays, modern thought is prone to seek its cause in heritage and early environment—frequently viewing the transgressor as less of villain than of victim—a sufferer from implacable circumstance. But thought that is modern today, you wisely will tell me, may tomorrow become ancient and outmoded. Assuredly, there comes a time when each man in his limited generation helplessly recognizes this possibility, and is terrified by the weakness of the transitory weapons of thought placed at his disposal. With such a feeling of fear, do I ask you, Saint Mark, concerning the parentage of Judas—speculating upon the influence it may have wielded upon that most tragic life. All that we know today, is that he was a native of the city of Kerioth in Judah—"Judas Iscariot" being translated, Judas of Kerioth— and that his father was named Simon.

It is emphasized to us that he was the only one of the Twelve not born a Galilean; the further speculation is thus fostered as to just how greatly this fact separated him from his companions in mentality and sympathy. Would it not seem almost certain, Saint Mark, that he, a native of different soil, steeped in different customs, could not have always seen eye to eye with the others—and that they, at times, must have viewed him as a stranger inappropriately in their midst? Yet had the Master chosen him, as He had chosen them, to be His friend and His disciple—and this alone should have swept away any barriers to congeniality.

I've often wondered, Saint Mark, if as some think it was really greed for money which tempted Judas into his terrible betrayal, whether the special office he held in that little company had not actually nourished that greed until it grew to such dimensions as to dominate him completely. For we are told that he carried the purse, and that only he was responsible for payment of all expenses incurred and alms dispensed in the Name of the Master and His Apostles. Thus money, the root of all evil, was constantly with him, and had of necessity to be much a part of his thought. The post of treasurer is never an enviable one in any organization. Its responsibilities induce very real temptations and obstacles in the path of spiritual progress.

We catch our breath over Saint John's words, almost brutal in their frankness, yet so clear that not the slightest ambiguity can be charged. Of course you know the chapter to which I refer—the one describing the supper which took place in Bethania, in that home which had shortly before witnessed the miracle which more than any other had won the greatest reverence of the multitude and aroused the deepest hatred of the Pharisees. The home of Lazarus, whom He had raised from the dead. There, we are told, He sat down to supper with His Apostles, and Lazarus and his sisters, Martha and Mary. By the miracle which had brought their brother back from death, the Master had shaken the very foundations of thought. It was no wonder the multitude, hearing that One sat within Who had literally called from the grave the master of that house, surged about its doors. Nor was it strange that the company gathered around that board should have been wrought to such adoration and awe that one, seeking an outward expression for these emotions, should have acted as she did.

"Mary therefore took a pound of ointment of right spikenard of great price, and anointed

197

the feet of Jesus, and wiped His feet with her hair: and the house was filled with the odour of the ointment. Then ... Judas Iscariot, he that was about to betray Him, said: 'Why was not this ointment sold for three hundred pence, and given to the poor?' Now he said this, not because he cared for the poor; but because he was a thief and, having the purse, carried the things that were put therein."

Terrible words, Saint Mark—yet I would ask you, had Judas perhaps turned thief only since money had become his special charge? Was it that sinister purse, ever at his side, which alone had discovered the weakest part of his moral nature, and had consistently eaten away at its roots until finally that portion had tragically crumbled? Yet, thief or no thief, tears dim our eyes as we read on further—how the Master, knowing all things to come, seemed yet to be striving to conquer with His love the destroyer ravaging that soul—that destroyer which had prompted Judas to spoken criticism of Mary. Gently He remonstrated: "Let her alone, that she may keep it against the day of My burial. For the poor you have always with you—but Me, you have not always." Was not this, Saint Mark, as much as saying: "Judas, Judas, I have so loved you—and you too, in your poor human way, have loved Me, and have striven to follow Me. Perhaps, if I say to you thus, that I am soon to die —soon to leave you—perhaps, dear Judas, your love will be rekindled, and you will reopen your heart to My grace."

Surely then, Saint Mark, as the Master looked pleadingly upon him,—surely some spark of the old love which had first led him to his Lord, must have glowed in his heart. But only briefly—for, alas, from that scene forward does the tragedy move on implacably, to its ultimate, terrible conclusion.

As you know, both Saint John and Saint Luke tell us that the devourer, Satan, at the end had completely mastered Judas. "And Satan entered into Judas, who was surnamed Iscariot," wrote Saint Luke. But you, Saint Mark, merely say: "And Judas Iscariot, one of the Twelve, went to the chief-priests to betray Him to them." It is as though you had been so horrified by the contemplation of such a development that you were too stunned to attempt any explanation of its cause. I have often wondered if it is not perhaps significant that in recounting that treacherous bargain, only Saint Matthew records the actual sum which closed it. He, like Judas, had once been much occupied with money, when, before the Master called him, he fulfilled his duties

as tax-collector for the conquering Romans—
and even though those days had long since passed
when he wrote his Gospel, it was not strange that
the recording of sums of money came naturally
to him:

"Then went one of the Twelve, who was
called Judas Iscariot, to the chief-priests, and
said to them: 'What will you give me, and I will
deliver Him unto you?' But they appointed him
thirty pieces of silver."

I often reflect, so unhappily, Saint Mark, on
the thoughts that must have possessed Judas in
those immediate hours after he had closed his
terrible contract. Was there not an inward strug-
gle to silence that wee, small voice which still
perhaps was urging him to return and revoke his
agreement before it was too late? Fearfully he
must have gazed about him as he left the court of
mighty Caiphas, lest any should be observing
him. A dangerous undertaking this was, as Saint
Luke so clearly implied when he wrote: "... and
he sought opportunity to betray Him *in the absence of the multitude.*" It must be done when
none of those who had recently strewn palm-
branches at His feet, singing "Hosanna to the Son
of David: Blessed is He that cometh in the Name
of the Lord!" were about. For surely they would
permit no harm to come to their recognized Mes-

siah. As he went his way, the chill hand of fear must have closed over the heart of Judas.

Soon after, did he not, Saint Mark, literally have to force himself to join the others for that last repast with Him? I shudder to think, when he reluctantly entered that chamber, how he must have avoided their eyes—and wonder, Saint Mark, if he did not attempt to sit as far as possible from the Master. But things fell out otherwise; and surely it was circumstance rather than Judas's own doing which placed him so close to his Lord at table that their hands should touch in the dish. Did not his heart miss a beat when, in a sudden lull, the voice of the Master rose clearly, sadly: "Amen, I say to you, that one of you is about to betray Me"? "And they," continues Saint Matthew, "being very much troubled, began every one to say: 'Is it I, Lord?' But He, answering, said: 'He that dippeth his hand with Me in the dish, he shall betray Me.'"

As though burnt by fire, Judas must have snatched back that tell-tale hand. Then, Saint Mark, was it not in the hysteria which overcomes people burdened with a sense of wrong-doing, and destroys all their caution, that Judas wilfully persisted: "Is it I, Rabbi?" And now his heart must have almost stopped beating when the Master replied: "Thou hast said it."

Why was it, Saint Mark, that both Saint Luke and Saint John refrained from quoting those terrible words which you and Saint Matthew set down as then being uttered by Him in reference to His betrayer? I scarce have the power to write them, so awful is their import: "It were better for him, if that man had not been born!" I almost wish, dear Saint Mark, that you, too, had refrained from recording them—yet, having been uttered, it was like you, whose symbol after all, is the symbol of courage—the lion—bravely to put them down, though you must have trembled as you did so. Surely Judas, hearing them, was as one in whom all rational mental processes were paralyzed—the grip of Satan upon his soul so strong, that at last he was powerless to do aught but what the Prince of Darkness commanded. Yet somehow I think he must have suffered terribly, helpless though he then was, when the Master turned pointedly to him, and said: "That which thou dost, do quickly."

And Saint John relates: "Now no man at the table knew to what purpose He said this unto him. For some thought, because Judas had the purse, that Jesus had said to him: Buy those things which we have need of for the festival day: or that he should give something to the

poor.—He therefore ... went out immediately.—
And it was night."

Night, indeed, for poor Judas—such a dark
night as his soul had never before experienced. I
think, Saint Mark, that he must have wept as he
stumbled helplessly along in that overpowering
blackness, led triumphantly by that arch-enemy
of the dear Master Whom he, Judas, had once,
and not so long before, so lovingly served. But it
was night—and in that terrible darkness was
the Prince of Darkness mercilessly wielding his
power.

Once again, as at the start of this letter, I
would lay down my pen, Saint Mark. I do not
think I can continue. Yet, concerning that awesome tragedy, there is still much more I would
ask. Perhaps, having gone so far, I may as well
conclude.

When Judas then had been swallowed up in
the darkness of that blackest night, behind him,
in that upper chamber where their Lord was
comforting the others as He bade them farewell,
a warm light must have shone. "Let not your
hearts be troubled," He was gently saying, even
as, in a far quarter of the city, the servants of the
chief-priests were arming themselves for His ap-
prehension. As you have related it, Saint Mark:
"And when they had said an hymn, they went

forth to the Mount of Olives. . . . Cometh Judas Iscariot . . . and with him a great multitude with swords and staves, from the chief-priests and the scribes and the ancients. And he that betrayed Him had given them a sign, saying: 'Whomsoever I shall kiss, that is He; lay hold on Him and lead Him away carefully.' And when he was come, immediately going up to Him, he saith: 'Hail, Rabbi': and he kissed Him."

Oh, Saint Mark—at that moment did not helpless Judas hear, close to his ears, the ironic laughter of the Fiend, mocking, that a kiss, the symbol of love, should thus bring the earthly downfall of Him Who was in truth the epitome of all love? And did it not seem to Judas as though a sword were run through his heart when he heard his Lord's gentle, sorrowful question: "Judas, dost thou betray the Son of Man with a kiss?"

I have often thought, Saint Mark, though timorous to voice an opinion where theologians have feared to tread, that perhaps it was that question, so fraught with pathos and the complete summation of his treachery, that first awakened Judas to the full realization of what he had actually done. From that moment forward, did not his suffering increase until he could no longer bear its agonizing pain, and until he was driven—but again, my own words fail me. After all, Saint Matthew has put it so much better than I ever could, were I to practise writing all the conscious hours of the rest of my life, that it's best simply to recall his narrative to you:

"And they brought Him bound, and delivered Him to Pontius Pilate, the governor. Then Judas, who betrayed Him, seeing that He was condemned, repenting, brought back the thirty pieces of silver to the chief-priests and ancients, saying: 'I have sinned in betraying innocent blood.'—But they said: *What is that to us? Look thou to it!*'"

Oh, Saint Mark—do you not think they were the cruelest of the cruel, these chief-priests? Do you not feel with me a great pity for Judas, striving desperately to undo the wrong whose profundity he only now perceived in all its horror? Now throwing himself on the mercy of those who had led and encouraged him into evil—those who, alas, knew no mercy? To me, those words seem the bitterest ever heard—"What is that to us? Look thou to it!" I weep for Judas, wrong though it may be, when I read: "And casting down the pieces of silver in the Temple, he departed—and went and hanged himself."

If, truly, the love of money had induced his temptation, naught of it remained when those thirty pieces of silver rang out so despairingly as they fell and rolled on that hard, cold marble floor—as hard and cold as the hearts of those he had just importuned. And how hypocritical were these same! For having just turned deaf ears to his plea, "I have sinned in betraying innocent blood," they picked up the pieces of silver, saying: "It is not lawful to put them into the corbona, because it is the price of blood." Did you ever hear of such two-faced psychology, Saint Mark?—"And after they had consulted together, they bought with them the potter's field to be a burying-place for strangers. For this cause that field was called Haceldama, that is, the field of blood, even to this day."

Dear Saint Mark, my hand is weak, my soul heavy with sorrow, as I conclude these suppositions on the heart-breaking tragedy of Judas. Nor am I any longer concerned with the various theories regarding his motives that have been advanced by mankind. I was, for instance, going to ask you just how it was that that early Gnostic sect, the "Cainites," came to the conclusion that Judas really acted consciously for the good of all mankind in betraying his Lord so that the world might be redeemed through His blood—and just how Origen had come to believe that poor Judas hanged himself in order to be the first of the

Twelve to meet Jesus in the other world, there to crave His forgiveness. And I was even going to ask you what you thought of the current modern belief that Judas, by his betrayal, only hoped to precipitate a political crisis which would force the Master into immediate establishment of an earthly kingdom, over which He should rule supreme.

But now, having dwelt again upon that terrible story, all explanations of its cause seem to sink into utter insignificance. My mind is too numbed to consider them—my eyes and my ears only are active. For do I not see, as though actually before me, that bleak cross on Calvary, its arms stretched wide in a gesture of love that would embrace all mankind? And do I not hear those pleading words coming from that suffering Figure nailed upon it: "Father, forgive them— for they know not what they do!"

Surely, Saint Mark, at that supreme moment—surely He, being truly God, was not forgetting Judas, His purse-bearer—Judas, the man of Kerioth.

AN EPISTLE TO SAINT PAUL

AN EPISTLE TO SAINT PAUL

D EAR S AINT P AUL :
For reasons I'd rather not go into, I am unable to address you in Greek, the language you always employed in letter-writing; but in spite of this, and even though my manner of salutation must seem to you somewhat abrupt, I hope you will read this letter with patience. There is so much I want to say to you; and I suspect that, were I to attempt the more dignified and infinitely more beautiful form of salutation which you used in your own letters, you would find me guilty of utter swank, and read no further.

I did try writing out: "Helen, an admirer, who wishes to become a friend, To Paul of Tarsus, greeting,"—and it looked too utterly silly—inappropriately "high-hat," for one in my graceless position in a graceless age. Yet, bizarre as it may seem, I have long been impelled to write you an epistle.

It will, perhaps, startle you to learn the desire was born of the suspicion that we shared at least two points in common—one, you were forever writing letters and nobody seemed ever to answer them; and two, you had a weakness for making puns (don't try to deny it). I wonder if people were always jumping on you, as they are on me, for this *petite faiblesse?* It's a dreadful admission of egotism to confess that, when I discovered your puns were almost as bad as mine, it drew me even closer to you than years of listening, each Sunday, to your beautiful Epistles. There is, for instance, that atrocious pun you perpetrated in your Epistle to Philemon when you asked him to take back and forgive his runaway slave, Onesimus, who had not only decamped but had robbed his master as well, but whom you had recently converted. Now, Saint Paul, in spite of my little Latin and less Greek, I do know that the name Onesimus is the same in Greek as the word for "profitable." Thus translating, you are discovered shamelessly writing to Philemon: "I beseech thee for my son, Profitable, who hath been heretofore unprofitable to thee, but now is Profitable both to me and to thee."

But though you couldn't resist a pun now and then, with what genius you wielded words and, through them, men! Never before nor since has been evidenced such a driving, glorious power in forging phrases and flinging them forth to accomplish the purposes of the Master Whom you served with such flaming love and undaunted self-denial—and for Whom you were, at length, to lay down your life, having "fought the good fight." Outwardly, indeed, you were a valiant warrior; inwardly, one who knew that serenity of an undivided love and purpose, which you defined so beautifully as "the peace of God which surpasseth all understanding." In the "armour of God, with the breastplate of justice, the shield of faith, and wielding the sword of the Spirit," you waged such a warfare with words as the world is likely never to see again. It is a fascinating oc-cupation to read in them precisely what method of attack you chose for the diversified citadels you set out to conquer—how, becoming "all things to all men, in order to save them," you phrased each epistle in the manner apt to touch most surely its recipient. I'm thinking of that same letter to Philemon. Wanting him to forgive the erstwhile thieving Onesimus, and reinstate him not as slave, but as brother (Philemon also being one of your converts) you wrote with un-erring wiliness:

"And if he hath wronged thee in anything, or is in thy debt, put that to my account. I, Paul, have written it with my own hand; I will repay it—*not to say to thee, that thou owest me thy own self also.*" That last shaft was what did it, Paul. How could the poor man refuse?

Of course, when I make the statement that you were always writing letters which remained unanswered, some may protest that certain evidence exists of your receiving correspondence. The Corinthians wrote to you—but, from what you say in reply, I don't think it could have been a letter which pleased you very much. On the whole, I feel certain you wrote far more and longer letters than you ever received. The marvel is that you had the time—for you certainly were one of those people to whom things were constantly happening. I can't think of you as ever having had a dull moment—so fraught with drama was your whole life as we have come to know it.

You've no idea how thrillingly spectacular your conversion (which really began your life) seems to us, living in this uninteresting century. What a fiery and militant Jew you were, Saint Paul, when, approaching Damascus with the set purpose of bringing imprisonment and death to its Christians, you were violently flung to the ground by that unseen Force, and stricken blind! I have lived over with you, many times, that greatest moment in your life when the Voice spoke to you—and instantaneously re-made your soul, your aims, and your entire existence. And I literally tingle at the thought of how drama continued to cling to you: "Of the Jews five times did I receive forty stripes—thrice was I beaten with rods; once I was stoned; thrice I suffered shipwreck, a night and a day was I in the depth of the sea—in perils of waters, in perils of robbers, in perils from my own nation, in perils from the Gentiles, in perils in the city, in perils in the wilderness—in perils from false brethren—in hunger and thirst—in cold and nakedness." And the last, final glorious drama—the headsman's axe descending, just beyond the walls of Rome.

What makes the story so human is that the drama was not infrequently mingled with comedy. Of course you remember the Christian, Ananias, in Damascus, who was told in a vision that he must baptize you, seeking you out in "the street that is called Strait." He seems to have put up strenuous objections. Was it because he was named Ananias, and the street was called Strait? He did capitulate, however, and it must have been a great relief to you to be properly baptized and to have your sight restored. But what a one you were for no sooner getting out of hot water than plunging into it again! Straightened out by Ananias, you began boldly to preach your new creed in Damascus; the authorities got after you, and you would have been popped right into prison had not the brethren secreted you. While the gates of the city were guarded against your escape, they lowered you in a basket from the walls! I often think of you, dangling precariously, praying the rope would hold.

Even though the joke was on you, Saint Paul, I think you will agree that there was comedy in your experience at Lystra, when you arrived with Barnabas to spread the Gospel. You certainly began with a superb gesture, crying to a life-long cripple: "Stand upright on your feet!" Whereupon, he "leaped up and walked." But do you recall how the astounded townspeople declared that only Jupiter and Mercury could perform such miracles; therefore, you must be Mercury (since you were chief speaker) and Barnabas must be Jupiter? They joyfully shouted: "The gods have come down to us in the likeness of men!" Naturally, you were somewhat taken aback. There they were, as a result of your miracle wrought to bring them a new religion, lustily cheering for the old! And when you saw a jubilant multitude preparing a nice sacrifice of oxen and garlands to lay at your outraged Christian feet, your consternation must indeed have been great. Poor Saint Paul!

Reading over your wonderful letters, it has struck me as perhaps unfortunate that they have come to be known as the "Pauline Epistles";

and some of them, as the "Pastoral" Epistles. Youth is woefully ignorant—and I know, rather too intimately, at least one person who, as a child, thought there must once have been a lady named Pauline who had been a great letter-writer—and who was sure the Pastoral Epistles dealt only with rural life. Bored with the two ideas, she investigated no further. Later, when an overdue enlightenment dawned on what you can see was a lamentable intellect, she was further deterred from studying them by the unjust charge that you were a violent anti-feminist. Not that I think the charge utterly groundless, Saint Paul. But that a careful reading of your Epistles indicates it has been grossly exaggerated, with no allowance made for extenuating circumstances. I can even see you, at times, a very sound feminist. You did not cheer too much for marriage in the first place (nor do our most modern feminists) but if entered into (you admit reluctantly that "it is better to marry than to be burnt") you uphold women's rights in the home, at least. "Art thou bound to a wife? Seek not to be loosed." Some of my sex have deemed it unfortunate that you saw fit to continue: "Art thou loosed from a wife? Seek not a wife." But I feel sure you would have stated the same precept to women, had you been addressing them.

As for your other alleged severities, tackling them as I do, a confirmed feminist, I think I can see a good reason for them all. Loath as I am to admit it—unique as your experience may seem —it must be conceded that women had given you no end of trouble. When you and Barnabas were going after the conversion of Antioch in a big way, and the Jews got the women of the town to arouse the authorities against you, it was the feminine clamor which caused your forced withdrawal. Also, there were those two ladies of your own Philippian Church, Evodia and Syntache, who, in that otherwise peaceful congregation, stirred up all kinds of dissension with their theological disputes. Even after all these centuries, their shrill arguments seem still to linger on the air. Their very names lay them open to suspicion. I can almost see Evodia pulling Syntache's hair, and Syntache scratching back. Your gentleness in rebuking them must have made them very much ashamed of themselves: "I beg of Evodia, and I beseech Syntache, to be of one mind in the Lord."

Did you know that the story has gotten around that there was also a damsel of Iconium —one Thecla—who caused you considerable embarrassment? It is related that she became such an ardent convert that she insisted on dressing up as a boy, with a view toward accompanying you on all your missionary journeys! There is only one word I can think of to describe adequately your state of mind at this juncture. You must, in fine, have been flabbergasted! With some difficulty, you succeeded in side-stepping her; but later, I'm sure, must have amply forgiven her when you learned she had braved martyrdom for the Faith.

Then there was that other lady who upset you considerably. You remember—the one who lived in Thyatira, and was possessed of a "pythonical spirit" which revealed the future to her. She "brought to her masters, much gain by divining." How it must have irritated you, whenever she saw you as you walked quietly in the public streets—for then, we are told, she would quit her job, run after you and tag you up and down the town, all the time crying out loudly your name and mission. "And this she did many days." No one can blame you, that this unwelcome publicity got to be such a nuisance that you finally had to turn in your tracks and exorcise the spirit possessing her. It was most unfortunate, Saint Paul, that this also had the effect of ruining her commercial value. The spirit gone out of her, her masters soon found she was no longer any good at prophesying. Naturally, they had you arrested for interfering with their business—and you were beaten and thrown into prison.

Ladies, all—and now after all these years, when you really should be allowed to continue, undisturbed, a well-earned peace from feminine botheration, here I come along with this epistle! Small wonder, that with a few such experiences, you felt like writing: "Let women keep silence in the churches—If they would learn anything, let them ask their husbands at home." (The less they bothered you the better.) I am a trifle encouraged, however, to read that women, if they lived long enough, might hope eventually for your confidence. You admonish Bishop Timothy, of the Ephesus Church, in selecting widows to help him, carefully to choose those not less than sixty years old. You take pains to add: "But the younger widows avoid." Since philosophers of succeeding centuries have concurred in the soundness of this caution, I'm sure Timothy must have seen the sense to it.

The fact that you had so many loyal women disciples and friends is ample proof that you were no unjust anti-feminist. Among these rarer women who seem to have given you no trouble at all, the most interesting must have been Priscilla, the wife of Aquila, the tent-maker. I like to think of how you met this charming married couple at Corinth, on one of your missions, and how they at once enthusiastically embraced your doctrine. Of course, you three had much in common, for you also were a tent-maker by profession, having learned the trade in Tarsus, your native city. It is interesting to us, living in this age of business, that although you were the son of wealthy and prominent Jews, who had given you a scholar's education and the proud birthright of Roman citizenship, you had also been taught this practical craft. It enabled you always to earn your own living. Independent and energetic, you fairly reveled in your tent-making —and when you found that Priscilla and Aquila were fellow-craftsmen, you abode with them, together assiduously plying the trade and spreading the Gospel. It must have been one of the happiest of partnerships, this sharing of manual work and a great spiritual, crusading Ideal. Then, too, since your friends were widely traveled (their business taking them frequently to Rome), this gave you further congeniality. Throughout your long life, their faithful friendship must have proved one of the happiest of the many you formed. From their names, they really must have been delightful people. One wonders if the early Christians, whenever they did fall into the weakness of matrimony, chose only mates whose names made a metrical blending with their own—and if Priscilla and Aquila were first drawn to each other because they "rhymed" so nicely?

But you had so many friends—too numerous to mention in this epistle. I hope it has long since ceased to distress you that occasionally you quarreled with some of them. You should remember that they were always quarrels arising from your conviction that your Master was not being well served—and usually were soon mended. Personally, I've had a difficult time forgiving you the hard things you said about Saint Peter, in reference to his not eating, when Jews were present, with the Gentiles. Even though he had shared their meals when you and he had been alone with them, I don't think you should have upbraided him. I, who understand Saint Peter better than you did at that time, know the poor man was only trying to follow one of your own precepts—to be all things to all men, in order to save them. If he openly ate with the Gentiles, he stood in danger of losing the Jews, his own people—and if he stumbled a little in his efforts to carry water on both shoulders, you should have been the last to blame him. But you had to go and write the Galatians all about it.

Saint Peter seems to have indulged his revenge only in the mildest and most saint-like manner: "Our most dear brother, Paul, hath written to you . . . in his epistles . . . in which are certain things hard to understand," was the gentle reflection he allowed himself. But since Peter seems to have forgiven you, and since you spent the later years of your lives laboring together for the Faith in Rome, there sharing the last same fatal prison, each to go forth from it to martyrdom, the least I can do is to brush away any lingering doubts.

And indeed I do, most sincerely, Saint Paul, when I think of the sadness and loneliness of your last imprisonment at Rome. An old man of seventy, abandoned by all your friends, the dreadful persecution of Nero having terrified them into flight, you faced your last days without the consolation of friendship—always your greatest earthly joy. Even the sole heroic friend, Onesiphorus, who "had not been ashamed of your chain," and had sought you out in prison, had to die before your own end came. You were, perhaps, the most extraordinary prisoner that imperial Rome ever saw. And what a disconcerting effect you had upon all your guards! In your first and less severe incarceration, you had been allowed to keep your own lodgings, and to preach—but every minute of those two years you were chained to a Roman legionary. I like the way you got even—by converting him. Under the circumstances, the poor fellow hadn't a chance!

There is still so much more I'd like to write you, Saint Paul, but I fear I've wearied you overmuch already with a story that is, in truth, an old one to you. And if Saint Peter happens to be looking over your shoulder as you read, you might tell him I hope, for "auld lang syne" at least, that he won't be quite so critical of my epistle as he was of yours. I'm very sensitive to what he may think of me—and, on second thought, I'd prefer it if you didn't leave this letter lying about.

P. S.—TO SAINT PAUL

P.S.—TO SAINT PAUL

SINCE writing you that epistle, Saint Paul, my conscience has been bothering me with the urge to supplement it with a postscript. You may be alarmed—in fact, I think you will be —in view of the usual masculine opinion of feminine postscripts. Too frequently are they suspected by your sex of not only being longer than the letters to which they are appended, but also of containing matter which properly belongs in these—facts generally upsetting to the orderly mind of the male. If it really weren't for my conscience, I'd forego the postscript. I deplore the former just as much as you must; only I can't seem to do anything about it. It keeps telling me, for instance, that in my letter, I did, after all, treat my own sex rather shabbily. Into detail I went, describing all the trouble that women had caused you during your lifetime—but I said very little about the greater trouble caused you by men.

We girls would like to have it borne in mind that in all your major persecutions, scourgings, and imprisonments, it was, of course, men who were responsible. They were the leaders of the synagogues, the high-priests, the centurions, and the governors. The Emperor who sat upon the throne of Rome, and who relentlessly pursued you and your contemporary Christians unto torture and death, was no lady, thank goodness. You can't deny that to all these can be laid the most tragic things which befell you. "For I will shew him how great things he must suffer for My Name's sake," the Vision had said of you to Ananias. But somehow I think that, like all mankind, you found the minor trials you underwent the most exasperating. Imprisonment and martyrdom you could meet with serenity; their very grandeur prevented them from exacting the heartbreaking toll wrung by, let us say, the continual experience of being completely misunderstood, even by your colleagues and friends.

At the very start, this bitterest of sorrows was to be dealt you by your masculine contemporaries. As you and I very well know (let's allow it to go no further) the Apostles themselves were the first to doubt you. It's perhaps bad taste to remind you, but you had really first sprung into prominence in Jerusalem as a robust and aggressive persecutor of the early Church. Commissioned by the high-priests, you set out to bring fire and sword upon these "Nazarenes," and, as with everything else you ever undertook, you accomplished the same with the utmost thoroughness. But suddenly and miraculously converted, you did a complete right-about-face; and immediately began, in Damascus, to preach the Faith just as exuberantly and publicly as you had formerly denounced it. You must admit that it was a startling reversal. The poor Apostles, sitting in Jerusalem and thinking each knock at the door was a summons to appear before the authorities and be tortured, were somewhat sceptical of your conversion. The more conservative of them (and you really could not blame them) seemed to have a little difficulty forgetting that you had looked on approvingly at the assassination of Saint Stephen, at which the "witnesses laid down their garments at the feet of a young man whose name was Saul; and they stoned Stephen." If these had only not checked their coats with you, the Apostles might have been more cordial. As you know, after that perilous descent in a basket from the walls of Damascus, you went to Jerusalem and "essayed to join yourself to the Disciples," but "they all were afraid." It must have been a most unfortunate position for you, Saint Paul. There you were, chafing at the bit to be off and evangelize in the name of the Master—and the Master's delegated representatives would have none of you. They regarded you as just so much poison-ivy.

Wasn't it fortunate that among the Disciples was Barnabas, who alone seemed to sense intuitively your burning sincerity? Having a sage eye the while upon the potentialities of your genius as a preacher, he at length convinced the little group, and you were accepted. But others there were, upon whom you depended, who, less justified than these, failed to understand you at all times. Isn't it true that this was, perhaps, the most sorrowful aspect of your life? For you were one possessing a remarkable capacity for friendship, and a great and obvious need of the sympathy of your fellow-men.

One thinks of John-Mark, the young kinsman of Barnabas, who, fired by your own enthusiasm, went forth with you and him upon that early missionary journey which was to include Cyprus and points on the mainland. It's very puzzling, Saint Paul. For from all that is recounted as happening at Cyprus, the sympathy of John-Mark should only have been augmented —for there, as you will recall, you wrought your first recorded miracle. Seeing in the Roman proconsul, Sergius Paulus, the possibility of a likely convert, you got to work at once. It must have annoyed you to discover, however, that he was somewhat under the influence of that cheap magician, Elymas, who used every means to prejudice his master against you. I like the way you fought him, in a sense, with his own weapons. As Elymas had been consistently throwing dust in the proconsul's eyes, you made the punishment fit the crime by actually (if only temporarily) blinding Elymas! Which was certainly rather neat. You made the magician's magic look, in the eyes of Sergius Paulus, like so much mumbo-jumbo—and so, you won your convert. But, somehow, you lost John-Mark. Now I wonder why he took himself off in a huff, and left you and Barnabas to continue the expedition without him? Poor Saint Paul, of course this defection disappointed you greatly; and what a pity that it had to bring even more distressing consequences!

Did you, I wonder, foresee them, when you proposed to Barnabas that second missionary journey? Was it a surprise to you that he would agree to accompany you only on the condition that you would also invite John-Mark? No one could blame you for refusing, after the latter's abrupt withdrawal before the first mission was completed—but how unfortunate it was that this caused your first quarrel with Barnabas, and one not to be mended for many years! With what anguish you must have seen this earliest defender and friend depart, with John-Mark, for Cyprus —leaving you to manage as best you might without them!

Then there was that other friend, who must have been with you for a time during your final imprisonment in Rome, of whom you sadly wrote in that last, pathetic Epistle to Timothy: "For Demas hath left me, loving this world." Nor was he the only one who abandoned you to the mercy of your Roman jailors and judges. Before these last, "at my first answer, no man stood with me, but all forsook me," you wrote to Timothy. (Your feminine admirers would have it noted that you did not write: "no woman stood with me.")

This fickleness on the part of some of your followers must not only have wounded your own faithful heart, but also have considerably hurt your pride. Don't deny, Saint Paul, that you possessed not a little of this very necessary quality. You had a justifiable pride, for instance, in being a "Jew of Tarsus in Cilicia; a citizen of no mean city"; and in being born to the high distinction of Roman citizenship. The latter, without doubt, got you out of many a tight scrape, and, I think you will agree, of itself played a dramatic rôle in your destiny. Even at the end, because of it, you could not be crucified or martyred in the other horrible fashions devised for Christians by Nero, but were sent instead to the headsman's block—the more merciful end meted out to convicted Roman citizens. (Not that I think the headsman's block was any cinch, Saint Paul—please understand me.)

Now, poor, dear Saint Peter, not belonging to your privileged class, and martyred at the same time—but I'd better not go into all that, lest my deplorable weakness for him lead me into a breach of tact.

Rather I would hasten on to tell you how you have always fascinated me, Saint Paul, by the methods you, the greatest evangelizer of all times, employed in making converts. It would seem as though you had literally stopped at nothing to win followers of Him for love of Whom you so gloriously labored, suffered, and died. I am thinking of that earthquake for which you lustily prayed—and received. Now some might claim that you wanted the earthquake only for the purposes of liberating yourself and Silas from the prison into which you had been unceremoniously thrust. But I know better. You had a designing eye upon the keeper of that prison. As convertible material, he struck you as rather impossible, and you determined that only something dramatic and terrifying could do the job. Falling on your knees, you besought Heaven for a nice earthquake (without casualties, of course) and lo—at midnight, crash, bang, the city began to rock, the buildings to crack and fall. The prison's trembling keeper, seeing the stout, stone walls come tumbling down about him, was immediately converted—as indeed, who would not have been? Receiving word at once from the authorities to free his obstreperous prisoner, he made haste to beg of you: "Go in peace." One earthquake was plenty for him—quite sufficient, thank you, to make him a pious Christian for the rest of his days.

When you attempted conversions *en masse*, men were, of course, constantly putting obstacles in your path. Of the various crafts which flourished in those days, I suspect you of being least sympathetic toward the metal-workers—for of your actual recorded quarrels, two seem to have been with such: Alexander, the copper-smith; and Demetrius, the silver-smith. You may recall that the latter enjoyed a lucrative business in Ephesus, where he made and sold silver temples to Diana, that lady being the most popular of all the Ephesian deities. Demetrius didn't like it a bit when you came along, preaching against graven images, and inducing thousands to turn a cold shoulder toward this Olympian belle. He found that you were woefully crippling his trade, and so, being a thorough business man, devised a clever scheme to quiet you. When he called that meeting of all the silver-smiths, he not only appealed to them on the common-sense ground of protecting their materialistic interests, but also cloaked his appeal with some sanctimonious-ness. "The temple of great Diana shall be reputed for nothing; yea, and her majesty... destroyed, whom all Asia and the world wor-shippeth," said he, virtuously. Quite up-to-date with some of our best twentieth-century business methods, were those of Demetrius. What a line! Wasn't it pitiful the way the people swallowed it, Saint Paul? Fired by his words, they captured two of your disciples and rushed them frenziedly into the theatre; and do you remember what a strenuous time the authorities had in quelling the tumult—and how they advised Demetrius to bring a suit against you, alleging restraint of trade? The upshot of it all being that you had to leave Ephesus, justified in the feeling you no doubt had—that Demetrius was no sterling sil-ver-smith.

Of other male Ephesians who must have irritated you greatly, there were those "seven sons of Sceva," the chief-priest, who, observing

the successful manner in which you cast out
devils, sought to plagiarize your method. You've
no idea how I've chuckled over the way they got
what was coming to them—how, entering in upon
a man "possessed," they cried to the evil spirit:
"We conjure you by Jesus, Whom Paul preach-
eth." But they couldn't fool the wily spirit. He
replied saucily: "Jesus, I know; and Paul, I know
—but who are you?" And he made a dive for
them, snatching and scratching. I'm sure they
regretted their impertinence as they fled,
wounded and naked, from the house.

An irrelevant thought makes me wonder
why, in your insatiable zeal for converts, you
didn't try introducing these seven sons of Sceva
to the four holy, prophetic daughters of Philip,
the deacon, in whose home you used to visit?
Perhaps regeneration of the seven might have
been thus accomplished. But I suppose you'll
say: "You're just like every woman—a match-
maker." Yet it does seem a pity, Philip having
four perfectly good, unmarried daughters, to
have ignored Sceva's seven sons, who, if not perfectly good at the time, might perhaps have become eligible Christian beaux if properly worked
upon.

But, after all, were not the gentlemen who
held the greatest malignancy toward you, those

"forty fanatics" of Jerusalem? You remember
that when you were in the custody of the tribune,
they gathered together and swore a solemn oath
neither to eat nor to drink, until they had killed
you. Of all the scurvy schemes—they requested
the chief-priests to ask the tribune to send you
again before the Council. The fanatics, meanwhile, were to lie in wait for you and kill you
before you ever reached that body. It was, indeed, fortunate for you, Saint Paul, that your
young nephew overheard the plot. When, breath-
less, he arrived at the castle with the news, the
tribune then and there made up his mind that,
as a prisoner and a Roman citizen, you were
rather too much of a handful—so he sent you
off by night, under military escort, to Felix, the
governor of Caesaria. I fear he was glad to be
well rid of you. And I should simply love to know
whatever became of the forty fanatics. They
never killed you, and if they literally fulfilled
their vow, they must have died of starvation—
but on this point, Scripture is disappointingly
silent.

On the whole, I believe that snakes were
kinder to you than many of your fellow-men.
There was that considerate little viper which lay
concealed in the fagots you gathered for a fire
when you were shivering from the shipwreck off

the Island of Malta. He sought the shelter of your hand, but nicely refrained from biting you. Had he done so, I shudder at the thought that the superstitious barbarians would have regarded it as proof that you were a murderer—and your life would not have been worth a nickel! As it was, they acclaimed you as a god, and showered honors upon you.

But of all the stories about you, Saint Paul, I think the most charming is the one concerning young Eutychus, the boy who fell asleep during your midnight sermon at Troas. You remember how crowded that upper chamber was, with people and smoking lamps. The only seat Eutychus could find was the ledge of an open window, and there he perched, and presently began to nod. "Being oppressed with a deep sleep, as Paul was long preaching ... he fell from the third loft down, and was taken up dead." A lesser preacher than you might have resented such a slight to his eloquence; but you immediately rushed down, and generously forgiving him all his snores, restored his life. Then you went back to continue your interrupted sermon until daylight. I often wonder if, in the course of it, you uttered that marvelously graphic exhortation to prayer you later used in your Epistle to the Hebrews: "Wherefore, lift up the hands that hang down, and the feeble knees." And did you, I should like to know, caution the brethren not to be "puffed up," a fault against which you were perpetually warning in almost all your letters? But I am almost sure, Saint Paul, that you admonished them to conquer "the old man," a foe to whom your Epistles constantly refer. That old man is just as troublesome today, as he was in your day—alas! Feminist as I am, I'm very glad you never made any reference to an "old woman" —no matter what you may have thought.

Somehow, of all the places I have followed you in thought, Saint Paul, I would rather have been in that upper room at Troas that night, than in any other. Your discourse must have been fraught with all the loving intensity of one who knew he was addressing for the last time his faithful followers, who in turn were unstintedly opening their ears and hearts to all their beloved teacher would say in farewell. We are told that on that memorable night, was held one of the first Eucharistic services, the brethren being assembled for the purpose of "breaking bread." With what holy reverence they must have bowed their heads, as you pronounced the words of Consecration!

But I have digressed somewhat from the purpose of this postscript—the enumeration of certain trials you underwent at the hands of the masculine sex, in an endeavor to lighten the black eye I gave my own. And now, a disturbing thought arises. It is the conviction that this detailed indictment of both your male and female enemies, will really greatly distress you—since, even though they are long since dead, it is a breach of your own beautiful precept. Too late I recall your Epistle to the Corinthians: "Charity is patient, is kind ... dealeth not perversely ... thinketh no evil; rejoiceth not in iniquity ... beareth all things, believeth all things ... endureth all things. ... For we know in part ... we see now through a glass in a dark manner; but then, face to face. ... Faith, hope, and charity ... but the greatest of these is charity."

After all, you needn't bother to reply to my letter and postscript, Saint Paul—for, indeed, I think you have already answered them.

WILL YOU TAKE THE CASE, DR. SAINT LUKE?

WILL YOU TAKE THE CASE,
DR. SAINT LUKE?

WHAT I present to you is, I'm afraid, quite a hopeless case, Saint Luke; but nevertheless because you are the only doctor at all equipped to handle it, I'm hoping you won't reply that you have long since given up active practice. Could you not make an exception this once, if only on altruistic grounds? For you see, it's strange—but my peculiar malady is one that does not cause me so much suffering as it does others who are totally disaffected. You'll admit, being a saint, that it's worse to cause others suffering than to suffer oneself. And you should admit, being a doctor, that any disease, however uninteresting, is worth an attempt to cure.

Unfortunate as it may seem, the truth is, Saint Luke, I would not be bothering you at all but for the fact that I've always admired you so extravagantly—not as physician only, but as individual. Of course it was your Gospel which first aroused my enthusiasm. From the moment I read it, I knew you were a very wonderful person; in fact, one of the greatest writers who ever lived. Have not many scholars affirmed that of those four inspired testaments, from a literary standpoint yours is, in many respects, the finest? Indeed, anyone with half an eye can see that it was written by a man of unusual culture—a sensitive poet and lover of beauty; for it contains certain exquisite touches omitted by the other Evangelists, but no less a true part of the Master's wondrous story.

For instance, in describing Saint Peter's unhappy denial of his Lord, while Saint Matthew and Saint Mark both state that when the cock crew Peter went out and wept, only you add the line which makes us understand just how sadly, deeply repentant was that great heart. I cannot refrain from recalling to you, Saint Luke, that passage so fraught with beauty which you wrote long ago:

"And when they had kindled a fire in the midst of the hall, and were sitting about it, Peter was in the midst of them, whom when a certain servant maid had seen sitting at the light, and had earnestly beheld him, she said: 'This man also was with Him.' But he denied Him, saying: 'Woman, I know Him not.' And after a little while, another seeing him, said: 'Thou also art one of them.' But Peter said: 'O man, I am not.' And after the space as it were of one hour, another certain man affirmed, saying: 'Of a truth, this man was also with Him: for he is also a Galilean.' And Peter said: 'Man, I know not what thou sayest.' And immediately as he was yet speaking, the cock crew. And the Lord, turning, looked on Peter. And Peter remembered the word of the Lord, as He had said: 'Before the cock crow, thou shalt deny Me thrice.' And Peter going out, wept bitterly."

In recounting these happenings, only you have given us the sentence: "And the Lord, turning, looked on Peter." Yet those words make the whole episode infinitely more vivid and poignant. Nor are they mere poetical embroidery; for, as we think upon that scene, an inmost conviction whispers: "Yes, surely, at that moment, his Lord must have looked on Peter."

Having been won, then, by the beauty of your Gospel, I began to search for information concerning you; and what fascinating things I learned! First, that you were a Greek, and born in Antioch—and that, like Saint Mark, while not one of His chosen Twelve, nor enrolling under His banner until after the Resurrection, still greatly privileged in being the close friend of His Apostles, and a pupil of perhaps the most powerful of all His followers—Saint Paul.

Both you and your great teacher seemed to

be forever writing; though how you had time for it with all the traveling and preaching you did together, is matter of marvel. We know, for instance, that, besides your Gospel, while modestly refraining from attaching your name, you did write The Acts of the Apostles—that wonderful record which is our only guide to the history of the earliest Church. It has struck me that you may have acquired the letter-writing habit from Saint Paul, for both these documents are actually written in the form of letters. And what wouldn't I give to know something of the person to whom they are addressed—that "most excellent Theophilus"! In your Gospel you salute him so charmingly:

"Forasmuch as many have taken in hand to set forth in order a narration of the things that have been accomplished among us; according as they have delivered them unto us, who from the beginning were eye-witnesses and ministers of the Word; it seemed good to me also, having diligently attained to all things from the beginning, to write to thee in order, most excellent Theophilus, that thou mayest know the verity of those words in which thou hast been instructed."

It would seem that you were a master of more than one art; not only a brilliant writer, but also, according to Nicephorus Callistus, an adept at painting. When I think of what a gifted and charming person you were, Saint Luke, I wonder that you succeeded in escaping matrimony—yet am forced to take the word of that ancient narrative, "Prefatio vel Argumentum Lucae," that you lived and died a bachelor.

But above all things does mankind know you best as a physician—a graduate, it is presumed by many, of the medical school of that famous university of Tarsus. Thus, who shall say, contemplating your life, that science, religion, and the arts are incompatible? It must have been a great comfort to those early Christians to have had a good doctor in their midst —and just how much it meant to poor, energetic Saint Paul, who was always shockingly over-taxing his physical frame, we can guess from his own words when he wrote to the Colossians: "Luke, the most dear physician, saluteth you." I love the way, Dr. Luke, your profession will out, even in the midst of your most artistic impulses; and I find it charming that in recording the incident of the sliced ear in the Garden of Olives, you are the only Evangelist to say a word about the cure of that ear! The others just leave us unpleasantly viewing that severed member dangling, as it were—but you, the doctor, were thrilled to report: "But Jesus ... said: 'Suffer ye thus far.' And when He had touched his ear, He healed him."

It is therefore, Saint Luke, as that "most dear physician" that I address you now.—No, I haven't the slightest ache nor pain; in fact, the trouble is wholly psychopathic. (Do I not begin like every patient, diagnosing my own case, rather than waiting for the doctor's analysis? It must seem like the old days, Saint Luke!) Symptoms? Well, to put it as briefly as possible, I seem possessed of an ungovernable inquisitiveness concerning things which are actually none of my business. And while you may say that curiosity has never been scientifically classed as a disease, I would remind you that it is said to have once killed a cat—and if a cat thus sickened and died, why not I? (I've given you a wonderful opening there, Saint Luke, but I know you're too much of a gentleman to seize it.)

This curiosity, while manifest from my earliest childhood, has increased alarmingly in the last few months. It has taken on a quality that I'm sure you'll admit is disturbing. For it has led me into fields where angels themselves might be arrested as trespassers; and has even recently tempted me into the impunity of writing inquisitive letters to the holy Apostles! I agree with you—terrible, indeed. Moreover, the gnawings of the malady, not even satisfied by this outpouring of queries, further led me into indicting questionnaires to Saint Paul and Saint Mark; and having gone so far, I saw no reason why you also should not be included. Particularly since it is you alone who possess the medical skill possible to cure me. And I'm sure, no matter what you may think of me, that you care enough for your friends to wish to see me healed. This invasion of their privacy, I think you'll agree, should at all costs be stopped.

But do you not think, the better to diagnose my case, that you should first permit me to question you? In that way you could best judge the extent to which I'm afflicted. And frankly, Saint Luke, I am literally suffering to interrogate you. If you could listen patiently, in the course of business as it were, I should be ever so grateful.

First I want to ask you why you didn't, in writing The Acts of the Apostles, give us a more detailed picture of the lives they led immediately following the Resurrection. And didn't the excellent Theophilus, when he received this communication, raise this same objection? For my part, I find it a little disappointing, for instance, to be led on by the delightful promise in that opening chapter, only to be let down so limply by your mere suggestion of that particular aspect. You get Theophilus and me all excited by what seems like the introduction of a truly fascinating subject; and then you plunge abruptly into totally different matters! These are very important, we agree—but quite incapable of stifling our curiosity regarding certain unmentioned details.

It is true that you begin very nicely by relating how the Apostles, having witnessed the Ascension of their Risen Lord, returned at His command to Jerusalem to await the coming of the Holy Spirit. "And when they were come in," you continue, "they went up into an upper room, where abode Peter and John, James and Andrew, Philip and Thomas, Bartholomew and Matthew, James of Alpheus, and Simon Zelotes, and Jude the brother of James. All these were persevering with one mind in prayer with the women, and Mary the Mother of Jesus. . . ."

Now right there is where Theophilus and I would have liked you to expatiate; but instead, you proceed at once with the appointment of Matthias to that twelfth apostolate left vacant by the tragedy of Judas. Of course we wouldn't have a word of that omitted—but how much we should have liked an amplification of the above! Please don't be offended, Saint Luke, for this is in no sense intended as a criticism of your magnificent literary ability. I've already told you what I think about that. But—well, I just can't help being curious about those first days in the upper room. For around the name of one of those whom you enumerate as being present, glows a very beautiful and mystical and (as with all things mystical) in part mysterious, light—revealing, yet unrevealing. It is the name of one whom we, knowing much, yet know too little—Mary, the Mother of Jesus.

Saint John tells us that, "having loved His own who were in the world, He loved them unto the end." It seems to me, Saint Luke, that her presence in that upper room was one of the most signal proofs He evidenced of that love for His own. For His Mother, though ever modestly in the background, had also been a faithful member of the little band which followed Him; and it would seem certain that, next to Him, in her they had found their surest guide, their most sympathetic friend. As for her Son, Who was her God as well as theirs, He had publicly shown His love for her on at least two occasions—at the wedding in Cana, where her thoughtful solicitude in saving her hosts embarrassment over the lack of wine induced Him, although His "hour had not yet come," to work His first public miracle; and later from the very Cross itself, when with almost His last suffering breath, He had tenderly commended her to the care of His most dearly beloved disciple, Saint John.

It pleased me so, Saint Luke, recently to learn that George of Nicomedia, writing in the ninth century, had explained His words on that occasion as implying that He was, in truth, commending her to all the Apostles; that when He said to John, "Behold thy Mother," He intended that though she was to be in the special charge of this disciple, she was actually to be a mystical mother to them all. Now I don't know another thing about George of Nicomedia; but at least his views on this subject coincide perfectly with my own. For I even suspect that the Master had left her on earth solely for the purpose of acting in this tender capacity to those dear, sorely bereaved friends. The epitome of the noblest motherhood He knew her to be—she who all His life had ministered so faithfully to His needs; she who when they murdered Him pitilessly, cruelly, had stood her ground so courageously—that ground, wet with His blood and her tears, directly beneath the Cross.

I like to think too, that in her own most terrible of sorrows, she in her way needed the Apostles. In spite of her great and mystical dignity, she was woman and mother; and their hearts must have been wrung with pity when they saw her, on that dark Friday, encounter Him on the Via Dolorosa; and when they watched her swoon at the sight of her Son bent beneath the weight of the Cross He carried.— "Spasmus Virginis"—the swoon of the Virgin— as it was inscribed on the long since vanished church supposed to have marked the spot, and revealed on a very ancient plan of Jerusalem. Have you not told us in your own Gospel how the venerable Simeon had many years before prophesied to the young Mother holding the Infant Saviour in her arms: "And thy own soul a sword shall pierce"? Of all the pictured and sculptured representations that have been made of the Passion-story, I ask you in your capacity of artist, Saint Luke, whether there are any, aside from those of the Crucifixion itself, more heart-rending, more evocative of compassion, than those of the Pietà—the sorrowing Mother grieving over the mangled body of her Son. And I am wondering whether you yourself ever made such a picture; for certainly there is tradition to the effect that you did paint her more than once. In fact, they have tried to ascribe the earliest portraits found (that in the Cemetery of Priscilla, those in the Catacombs, and even the later Byzantine ones) to you; a deduction which I suspect, were you not such a great saint, you might have resented—since I understand they are not considered particularly good, nor representative of any but a conventional type. For my part, I prefer to think that what pictures you made of her were lost—more's the pity for art, and for her devoted children here below.

Since pictures are such perishable things, how much I wish you had written, in your two great documents, more of her! When you stated: "All these were persevering with one mind in prayer with ... Mary the Mother of Jesus," could you not have explained how she took care of them in those first bewildered days in the upper room? Did she not, Saint Luke, fulfill with the utmost wisdom and tenderness her charge of mystical motherhood? Somehow it's so pleasant for me (earth-child that I am, with vision too narrowly bound to earth-things) to think of her smoothing out all their little human difficulties. I can see her with John, for instance, her most special obligation, acknowledging with many loving acts his staunch protection, yet not neglecting to curb his youthful impetuosity when it threatened to run away with him. And of course she loved Peter dearly (who could help it?) and may have advised him frequently in his weighty responsibility as leader of the infant Church. Perhaps sometimes he even gave her a little trouble over his sartorial carelessness (that way he had, only shortly before, of plunging into the water with all his clothes on!) yet must she have had to smile indulgently as she smoothed and mended the wrinkled garments.

I suspect, too, that she often aided James in straightening out his fishing tackle; and perhaps helped Andrew stitch up a torn sail, even though she may have had, the while, to restrain him gently in his match-making proclivities. For I can easily imagine that he might have tried to induce Philip to "marry off" his three daughters; and that Our Lady had to comfort the troubled father by assuring him that it wasn't at all necessary. As for Thomas—her specially devoted Thomas—I can see her affectionately defending him from the protests of the others over his occasional tardiness. And when it came to Bartholomew, I think she must have been very proud of his immaculate appearance, and probably aided him in all sorts of ways to keep that lovely white garment spotless.

How could she have helped being sympathetic and indulgent with Matthew in his weakness (always of a nice, modest, Apostolic kind) for giving parties?—And for his pure soul and his high courage, I'm sure she loved James the Bishop; though she may have had to urge him at times, for his own good, to be less self-effacing. The quiet, unobtrusive Simon must have been a great comfort to her—I often wonder if he, being an expert in leather, perhaps didn't fashion the sandals for her feet. As for Jude, who had such a gift for phrasing psalms of praise to their Lord, I'm certain she often asked him to lead that reverent little company in their devotions; but suspect that sometimes she may have had to restrain his evangelical zeal—those were dangerous days, and he *was* such a one for assuming the most monumental tasks!—

Now can't you see, Saint Luke, how Theophilus and I would have loved it, had you expanded in the Acts, that particular paragraph? But perhaps, after all, I'm not being fair to Theophilus. For I have no actual assurance that he was afflicted with the same unpardonable curiosity which is mine. He may have been a nice, uninquisitive person, for all I know. Alas, that my own malady in that direction is so pronounced, even were you to satisfy all the queries I have already put, I would still insist on pressing you further! I should so love to know, for instance, where Our Lady spent her last years— whether in Ephesus, as some maintain; or as the majority believe, in Jerusalem. Of course always she must have been with Saint John (except when he had to be off evangelizing) for his Gospel explicitly states that on receiving that solemn charge from the Cross, "from that hour the disciple took her to his own." And what do you suppose, Saint Luke, led Bar-Hebraeus, that thirteenth-century Jacobite bishop, to believe that she accompanied him on his exile to Patmos? Not that I think she wouldn't have gladly done so (do you recall that charming apocryphal letter, in which she graciously promises Ignatius to journey with John to visit him?) but that the accredited opinion is that she left this world before his exile, expiring at last from love and the desire to be reunited with her Divine Son, in the year A.D. 48.

You will understand, Saint Luke, why I particularly am drawn to the account of her passing, as given in the apocryphal "Falling Asleep of Mary." For therein it is related how dearly she held the Apostles. Lying on her couch, she prayed: "My Lord Jesus Christ, Who didst deign through Thy supreme goodness to be born of me, hear my voice and send me Thy Apostle, John, in order that seeing him, I may partake of joy; and send me also the rest of Thy Apostles, both those who have already gone to Thee, and

those in the world that now is, in whatever country they may be, through Thy holy command-
ment, in order that having beheld them, I may
bless Thy Name, much to be praised."

She would not pass from this world without
looking a last time upon the beloved faces of
these, her spiritual sons. Accordingly, "the Holy
Spirit said to the Apostles: 'Let all of you together, having come by the clouds from the ends
of the world, be assembled ... by a whirlwind,
on account of the Mother of Our Lord Jesus
Christ; Peter from Rome, Paul from Tiberia,
Thomas from Hither India, James from Jerusalem.'"

You yourself, though already dead and
buried, were not forgotten, Saint Luke—for
the account continues: "Andrew ... and Philip,
Luke, and Simon the Cananaean, and Thaddaeus,
who had fallen asleep, were raised by the Holy
Spirit out of their tombs."

Having been quite dead for some time, were
you not startled, not to say apprehensive, when
thus summoned? And was not this why the Holy
Spirit reassured you, saying: " 'Do not think that
it is now the Resurrection; but on this account
you have risen out of your tombs, that you may
go to give greeting to the honour and won-
der-working of the Mother of Our Lord and

Saviour, Jesus Christ, because the day of her departure is at hand—of her going up into the heavens' "?

And don't you love, Saint Luke, the way the narrator naïvely adds, as a sort of after-thought: "And Mark likewise coming round, was present from Alexandria"? But he seems to have completely forgotten Matthew, the other James, and Bartholomew! Yet I am sure you would tell me that these also were privileged to witness the passing of her who had, in those early years, ministered so faithfully to them all. For this they loved her devotedly—but above all, because she was the Mother of their Lord—she of whom one of them was later to write: "a woman clothed with the sun, and the moon under her feet, and on her head a crown of twelve stars. . . . And she brought forth a Man-Child, Who was to rule all nations."

Now I also wish you would tell me, Saint Luke—but there, I seem to hear you cry: "Enough! Let us get back to the matter of your ailment." You've really been very patient.—A serious case of exaggerated curiosity, you say? And I think I hear you prescribe longer and more frequent prayers. All right.—But do I also hear you forbid any more letter-writing? Oh, dear Dr. Saint Luke, couldn't you soften that a little?

It will be hard to give it up completely. I'm afraid it's become a habit. Now, if all my most delightful friends didn't live at such a distance—!